For Lou
What
WLST! Go, Wahoos!
Evie

His Name Was Donn

My Brother's Letters from Vietnam

Evelyn Sweet-Hurd

Outskirts Press, Inc.
Denver, Colorado

Dedication

For Phil, Caitlin, and Jeff

Acknowledgments

I want to thank my husband, Phil Hurd, for many years of love, encouragement, and support.

Thank you to my two first readers, Caitlin Hurd and Suzanne Carroll Pace, for their careful and considered reading, their input, and their very much needed enthusiasm for this project.

Thank you to Jeff Hurd, for his stimulating conversation and for sharing some of his knowledge about history and warfare, and for providing some of the best culinary experiences in the world as I worked on this book.

And thank you again to Caitlin, for lending her graphic design expertise to the cover of this book.

"Hello to everyone who reads this."

--Lt. Donn Sweet
Hill #23, Vietnam
November 7, 1967

Foreword

I am not at all sure I can do this. I have thought about trying for at least ten—maybe twenty—years. But I have never so much as put a syllable on a page. Unless you count the poem, which, I must say, I think is a very good poem. I wrote it more than ten years ago, and it won a $50 prize in a not very reputable poetry competition. Still, it made it into print, and I felt good about that. I had expressed a little of what I had been feeling since 1968. I suppose you could say that it was like someone feeling a snowflake on her cheek and saying, "Yes, there is a glacier somewhere."

It is odd how we drag certain things around with us for most of our lives. I have a saddle that I bought in 1970. I had a horse for about a year, or maybe a year and a half. I had to give the horse away, but I have kept the saddle, moving it with me from Virginia to Texas to Georgia, never using it again, but always thinking I might want to. I guess it is a touchstone for all of the parts of me that connect to horses, from childhood to the present.

In our most recent move, in June of 2006, I pondered again the saddle and things I had known equine. I doubt my knees will ever allow me to mount a horse again, much less try to ride. But the bigger question concerns another touchstone-- or is it a Pandora's box? It is most definitely a box. A box ill-suited to its task of holding letters and a few other items. The cover of the box doesn't even fit on the box, lending it a disheveled rather than a sacred appearance. But this box is my ark, it sometimes seems. I cannot get too close to it. I need to stay a respectful distance from it. I have peeked in it a time or two, and I have had a few signs that tell me to embrace it. It is a box of my brother's letters from Vietnam.

I don't know what is in those letters right now. I pulled one out and read a piece of it as I was moving the box around from its last home to its current place. I was surprised at it contents. I knew I needed to read more. I made a firm decision to organize the letters chronologically when we moved. The move is complete. The letters are untouched.

I'm sure it is indeed possible for me to die today at age 57. It would not be all that shocking, as people my age die every day. And so I ask myself if I want to die without having written about Donn. And the answer is no.

In trying to figure out how to approach this book, I lay in bed this morning, with my ridiculously sore knee propped on a pillow. I have in our new bedroom a Morris chair that has been in my family forever. I am not great at remembering my childhood, but that chair is in a lot of scenes. It has a ladder back, and a slim stick of wood that props that back up to hold the cushion up to form the back of the chair. As little kids, we would take that stick out and allow the ladder to lean to the floor, forming a perfect spot for a tent or a fort. I loved that chair, with its wide broad arms and its ladder back and its sturdy but not scary legs. I love that chair still. So today I imagined my brother sitting in it, looking at me. I watch way too many episodes of "Cold Case" on TiVo, and no doubt that is why I imagined Donn sitting in the chair and then kind of vaporizing, as the characters almost always do at the ends of episodes of that TV show. Those characters have died, and they revisit the detectives who have somehow put their deaths into some sort of perspective, allowing the police to write "closed" on the evidence box and the significant others of the characters to have some sense of closure.

I have pretty much given up on the idea of closure. But I still like the concept.

In searching for a muse to help me write this book, I have found one in my daughter. She is a freshman in college this year, and she is seventeen years old. We have always been able to talk about anything and everything, and I miss those conversations that would spring up unannounced as we would be driving to get some ice cream at Brusters or when we were leaving a place after she had introduced me to my very first pedicure.

Through the years she has learned bits and pieces about my brother, and one day she said, "I wish I could have known him. It would be fun to have an uncle like that."

I wish she and her brother could have known him, too. Caitlin would laugh and enjoy his antics, and Jeff would appreciate the sharp wit and humor. I can see Jeff and Donn sitting across the room from each other, enjoying Jon Stewart and Stephen Colbert, playing off of their zany intellectual takes on the news. Donn was a big fan of George Carlin, and Jeff has that same sense of humor.

Yes, they should have known their uncle. He was an amazing guy who lived a very full twenty-six years before he was killed in Vietnam. It is time for me to open the box, look at that familiar handwriting, and begin.

Life on a Day in March

Today I discover that I have small seashells in my
    jacket pockets
And I see again two children, flying a kite
        Running into icy ocean water
Laughing when the wind whips the dunes' sand
        Into their shining, fine hair.
In class today a young college student portrays Mr.
    Krapp
        (Beckett's own man)
And I see my brother as he must have been thirty years
    ago
        In college, young, lean, restless, dynamic
But wrenched from the university
        And extinguished in Vietnam.
        Mr. Krapp.
I finger the seashells in my pocket
Wondering if their worn smoothness holds some
    ineffable answer.
As my fingers massage the worn curves
I think of the ocean and time
Wearing away gently, steadily
        The rhythm of the universe gradual, even
        meaningful
When an unexpected bit of sharp shell tears the tip of
    my finger
Dark blood pours blindly in my pocket
Rendering my knuckles and hangnails murderous.
        ES-H, ~1995

Introduction

I have organized the contents of the box. I think I may take a picture; I am that amazed that I have been able to get this far.

There are letters and a few sundry items and a few official documents and too many telegrams. I did not even realize that telegrams were a part of the story; I thought that process of notification was history by 1968. Apparently not.

It is hard to know whether to start with the postmortem items. Hit you with the pain right upfront, to lend a different perspective to the living voice you will discover in the letters. Or should I stay with the chronology, the linear time that we lived. After all, he did not realize which letter would be the last letter, it just was. And we did not realize what letters would arrive in Vietnam too late, the ones that would be stamped "Search search search search" and returned to us unopened. I do not know where those are.

The box is missing things. I know I mailed his birthday letter too late; I had drawn goofy flowers on the envelope; it came back to me with "Search search search" and something about unable to locate. I have no idea where that letter is.

None of the letters in the box are to me individually. I am guessing that I discarded them, one at a time, haphazardly, in an assortment of college trashcans. It never occurred to me that he would not come home. It never occurred to me that his letters would be his voice on the page for me to revisit.

I am thankful to my mother for having the sense to keep her letters and a few other items. After the two gentlemen from the Army visited our house to tell us of Donn's death, I was all for destroying everything. Not just the reminders of the military; everything in the universe. I was Thomas Hardy's "Hap," shaking my fist at the universe and not knowing if any god or God could hear me. I would have destroyed everything, the memorial flag, the letters, the dog tags, the items returned as his personal effects. I would have burned them all in the huge fire of my anger. Is it the people of India who used to pile up the bodies and set them aflame? I would have piled up all the evidence of his life, thrown myself on top, and set it on fire.

Letter 1

Postmarked Lawton, OKLA, Sept. 25, 1966.
Return address:

O/C Sweet; BTRY D-1, OCS; Fort Sill, OKLA.

Sat

Hi Toombie,

It's a warm Sat afternoon and I received your Tillie the Typist letter today. Ta-ta.
Glad to hear Tony is enjoying better living conditions in Viet Nasty.

I sent Stu a card this past week, hope he got it.

I hope Dockie is being absorbed in the hectic life of a U of Wis coed, then she won't miss Joe so much.

With Joan's tape recorder you ought to record Suzanne's questions about the origin of babies. That (your answers) ought to be a riot.

I'd say that it would probably be too warm for a wool suit. (I'm not sure.) The temp. in the day is around the low 80s. At night it can get into the 60s. The last ceremony is the graduation exercise Tues (the 11th) at 10 a.m.

I really enjoyed the Polaroid prints. Mucho gracias.
Take care kids and see you soon.
Me

P.S. I trust C. told you about my assignment to Ft. Benning. I'm very pleased, it could have been Korea.
P.P.S. Dig the cards? (mandatory)

§§§§§§§§§

A few words here about names. Donn called our mom a variety of different nicknames. The one most frequently used in the letters is Toombie, a name he invented. He called her "Toombie" because he was afraid her weight was going to send her to an early grave. Now that she is 95, we know he was wrong about that. He called me Dockie because I was very thin in high school and he knew that his reference to a concentration camp—he even spelled it "Dachie"-- made me furious.

This first letter is addressed to my mother and my older sister, Joan. In the fall of 1966, I was a freshman at the University of Wisconsin. Joan and her daughter Suzanne had moved home to Roanoke, Virginia, while Joan's husband Tony was in "Viet Nasty."
The first postscript of this letter refers to C., who was Donn's wife, Carolyn. As teenagers, Donn and

Carolyn had eloped. Carolyn was a senior in high school, and Donn was in college. Their romance was passionate and intense. I remember thinking in my college Shakespeare class that Donn loved Carolyn like Othello loved Desdemona.

Carolyn was a very pretty, very sensual, very bright girl, and I admired her totally. She was what every high school girl wanted to be, in my mind. She even played golf and had her name in the paper. I was younger and quite in awe.

After Donn's death, I spent some years thinking that he must have died because his heart was broken and he didn't care any more about living. Carolyn had indeed shattered his heart before he went to Vietnam. But at the time he wrote this letter from Fort Sill, he and Carolyn were together, and the invitation to his graduation from Officer Candidate School was coming in the mail, complete with formal name cards. One said Donn Lafayette Sweet, Lieutenant, US Army. The other said Mrs. Donn Lafayette Sweet. The formal invitation is addressed simply in Donn's handwriting to "Toombie et al." No doubt he cackled with glee at the juxtaposition of the familiarity of that greeting and the formality of the embossed graduation invitation.

Letter 2

Postmarked Columbus, GA, June 1967.
Sent Air Mail for 8 cents.Postage due 8 cents.

FRI

Hello Toombie,

Thanks for the letter I received today. I might drive to Atlanta tomorrow to see Joan, I'm not sure yet. Steve might come up this weekend so I'm undecided right now.

I think it's just real top drawer that you started hanging out at Papa Joe's. That's class.

I have made a deal with the doctor here that owns the Porsche: He is going to sell it to me on the twentieth of June for $2200. I think that's a fair price, especially since I can sell it for $2500. without much trouble. Anyway it's what I want and I feel fortunate to get it at such an early date. Due to the fact that it's a used car I can not get a bank loan for the full amount therefore I have to put up something as collateral for the balance. My life insurance policies would be sufficient. The way it works is this: The bank holds my policies liable for the amount of the balance in case I should refuse to pay my loan back or if I should die. Therefore if I should use $600 of my life ins as collateral and within two years die, then the life ins company would pay the bank $600 and you and Dachau (the beneficiaries) $19,400. Understand? The thing is that for me to put the policies as collateral I have to own them, so will you please sign them over to me? Just sign both of the enclosed forms where the "x" is and return them to me PDQ and Air Mail. Any questions?

When do you expect to come down here? Anytime is all right with me for Dockie to pick up the MG. I can manage for a week or so. We were planning a wild party the tenth of this month, but I don't think it will come off as scheduled. Time will tell.

If you go to Sch'dy be sure to call God and Scott &/or Sukie. Pat G. should have delivered by now. Ask what it was. Tell them I expect orders before July first, but of course I can't be sure.

Take care and send the forms right away because they have to go to the company before I can get my loan.

Ta Ta,
Me

§§§§§§§§§§

Donn was at Fort Benning, Georgia, when he writes this letter in June of 1967. Our sister Joan, her husband, Tony, who had returned from Vietnam, and their daughter Suzanne lived in Atlanta.
Our dad died in 1961. Our mom never remarried.

Apparently in 1967 she went to Papa Joe's, a place none of us can remember now.

This letter introduces you to one of the major loves of Donn's life: his 1962 356 Super 90 Porsche. One of those old pearl-white Porsches that had kind of a bloated shape. Donn would not approve of that description. He thought this car was the definition of beauty itself. He named his car Patti Porsche, and he often referred to her as The Marshmallow. It was a great car, and I tried for many years to give it the love that Donn would have given.

Before our move to Roanoke, Virginia, in 1955, our family lived in Schenectady, New York. I recall that move vividly, as people from New York at that time were a little wary of what life might be like in the South. I remember my second grade teacher teaching me how to "write cursive," as she told me that Southerners wrote that way and I had better be prepared. Now, when I read Donn's letters, I see the Empire State style of penmanship: his letters are written in a printing style.

Upon our move to Virginia, Donn entered the ninth grade. Now that I have raised a couple of children myself, I realize what a year the ninth grade can be for kids. At the time, I just thought he was my older brother who was pretty much the smartest and funniest guy in the world. When he came home from high school with a bloody nose for announcing to the guys there that they were standing on conquered ground, I knew that he thought he was being funny with that comment. Some of his new Virginia peer group thought otherwise.

This second letter mentions some good friends that Donn had in Schenectady. "God" refers to Howard Goldstock, husband of Pat G. Howard and Donn were the best of buds, even though Howard was a few years older. I remember Howard coming up to me at Donn's funeral and he nearly fainted. I didn't realize that in the years since we had moved to Virginia, years I hadn't seen Howard, I had changed a lot physically. The little Evie who had moved to Virginia when she was starting the third grade was nineteen years old. And my face was now the spitting image of my brother.

§§§§§§§§§

As I approach the next letter, I feel the need of a writing coach. Or maybe an ethics coach. Or a spiritual advisor. Something.

With non-fiction, and in working with letters, life can be raw. Some people will hurt, and I don't want anyone to hurt anew. It has certainly been bad enough to hurt the way our family has hurt since July 25, 1968. It is impossible for me to know how my sister has hurt in those years. It is impossible for me to feel the pain that my mother has borne. One time just a few years ago, sometime around 2000 or 2001, my niece

Suzanne asked me if I knew that her mom, Joan, still cries often about Donn. No, I had not realized that at all. And our mother? When I asked her once about Donn, she replied, "He was just somebody we knew once." If the Biggest Defense Mechanism in the Universe Award should go to anyone else, please let me know. But it has worked for her; she has lived a full and vibrant 95 years, 38 of them after the death of her son.

So this next letter has some hurt in it. Should I leave it out? Or leave parts of it out? Or make a rule now about what I will and will not include? I haven't read all of the letters in the box yet, so there will undoubtedly be more hurt in there. But I have decided this is life as Donn recorded it. And if we can't see his anger, if we can't see his entire life because we are afraid to hurt, we need simply to close the box again and go away.

Letter 3

Postmarked Atlanta, GA, Sept. 11, 1967.
Mailed for 5 cents.
Envelope addressed to Mrs. A.L. Sweet + Dockie.

Thurs nite

Hello Family,

It's a sunny day here and I'm about to go over to Woody's and enjoy another nite on the town. Actually all I really want to do is to get out of this household. E-gad, you wouldn't believe the tension in this apt. Then, to top it off Joan came home from work tonite and said, "Here's your money for the refrigerator." It was supposed to be $125.00. She gave me $80. Said since it cost her $40 to have it shipped up here that's all I should get. Then she informed me that Tony was mad because he thought the refrig. was a gift! I said --- -------well, forget what I said. I guess I best take the $80 and run.

Needless to say I want you to sell my air conditioner next Spring for anything reasonable but NOT to J&T. G.D. they have a nerve! Besides that they seem to always bitch at one another. Whew!

Kathy comes up tomorrow and stays thru Sun. I'm going back to Columbus with her and flying back to Atlanta Mon or Tues nite.
I leave Atlanta Wed morn at 10:20 (I think) and fly to Seattle and points west.

Today I got the movie film in the mail and it's pretty good. I'll send it up to you. The 3 girls in the film you won't recognize are Judy, Kathryn, and Boots.

Yesterday I went over to Ft. MacPherson (sp) and ordered some new glasses. Hope to get them in about a month.

How are things going up there? What's new?

I'm glad I came to J&T's before leaving for Vietnam because now I won't mind leaving civilization (?) for the war.

Well, take care and give The Marshmallow a kiss for me. I think you two should be real Porsche converts by next year, yes?

Affectionately urine,
me'n

P.S. Fri—Had a call from Joan this A.M.…..said she thought she'd pay me $100. Wowee!!!

Letter 4

Postmarked Tacoma, Wash, Sept. 16, 1967.
Return address reads Lt. Sweet, 1948 Walmann Rd.,
Roanoke, VA 24018.
Addressed to Toombie Sweet.

Fri 15 September

Hello Toombie,

By the time you get this letter I assume Dockie will be at Duke. Be sure and write me about that and her roommate.

I arrived in Seattle Wed afternoon after a very nice flight. I took movies out the plane's window of Mt. Ranier. Wed nite I stayed with Gene C. and wife in Seattle. How about that? Gene is teaching and working on his PhD in math. It will take him at least 2 yrs to get it. He has a cute wife and they were very hospitable. He's very odd, I guess------his hair is long and shaggy like an educated hippy.

Thurs I arrived here at Ft Lewis. I was issued my jungle fatigues, boots and olive drab undies etc. Since I had no place to put it (in my bag) I'm having my old stuff sent home.

13

Tomorrow (Sat.) I fly on a chartered, commercial jet to Vietnam. The plane will probably stop at least once to refuel--- either Okinawa or Japan. We arrive in Cam Rahn (sp) Bay and from there I go to Dong Ha. I'll keep you posted.

How are things with you? How do you feel? Did you get the movies? How's the Marshmallow?

Well, that's about it for now. Take care and I'll write again as soon as I have something to report.

Love—
George Hamilton

P.S. "Wha happened?"

Letter 5

Postmarked Air Force Postal Service, Sept 26, 1967. In Donn's handwriting, the word FREE where the stamp would be on regular mail. The return address reads Lt Sweet, B BTRY 1st BN 40 ARTY, APO San Francisco 96269. Addressed to Mrs. A.L. Sweet.

25 Sept

Hello Toombie,

It's now 4:45 AM and I'm sitting in the FDC bunker supposedly learning what goes on. Actually I'm not doing much of anything. I've been assigned to B Battery as a forward observer. Big deal!

Currently this btry is located in Dong Ha which is base camp. Within two weeks we'll probably go to a place west of here called 'The Rockpile.'

There are 5 officers in this btry—2 of us are FOs. The other FO is currently out with a detachment of the South Vietnamese Airborne unit. From time to time I'll be going out with them and the Marines.

24 hours a day this place is in action. Our guns fire frequently. About 2 times a day we have a 'blue' alert

15

which means we're being shelled and therefore we have to get in a bunker. At all times we're required to wear a flak vest and steel helmet.

Dong Ha is a fairly big complex. We have the HQs at the HQs of the 12th Marine regiment. Here plus another battery and a small air strip.

Life here is rather uncomfortable and very dirty. The weather is wet and the mud is plentiful. I get to take a cold shower once every 2-3 days. In case anyone asks I could use some of those towelettes or whatever you call those things that you can wash with—without using water. Of course what I really want is mail.

Before too long I'll finish a roll of movie film and have it sent to you. The movies are a hodge-podge of quick shots but maybe you'll get an idea of what it's like here. Now, please find out if you can get my 16 mm Minox-type film developed there (prints-color) (36 to a roll). Ask John G. where would be the best deal. Avoid retail prices if possible. I'll send you a roll soon. After they are developed (I hope they come out ok) wrap them in plastic and send them to me. I'll label them and return them. You have to protect them from sticking to one another because of the heat and humidity.

Actually life over here is pretty lousy and the war is way too close for comfort.

From the Rock Pile we go to Gio Linh which is right next to Con Thien on the DMZ. That is a real hot seat. In the last month we had 2 of our guns knocked out with direct hits. The enemy here is the NVA (North Vietnamese Army) and they are well equipped and well trained. Too, they are here in strength.

Right now we're on a 72 hr alert which means Dong Ha is expecting a massive attack and thus we can't take our clothes off and must carry our M-14s (no M-16s up here yet) plus 100 rounds of ammo wherever we go. I'm the team leader for the 12th Regiment Reaction Force while we're here at Dong Ha. That means if and when we're attacked I take my 20 man team to the place that's catching the most hell and reinforce them. It's all rather hairy.

I'm trying to adjust to drinking something other than milk but not having too much luck. We get no liquor up here and are rationed one beer (hot) a day and one soft drink. The food isn't too bad.

I sleep in a tent on a bunk with an air mattress (no regular mattress available). I have a mosquito net and a sleeping bag.

If possible I'd like you to end the war so I can go home. Ta-ta.

By the way send me that sweat suit when you get a chance.

Besides the NVA we have scorpions, centipedes (up to a foot long), rats (up to one and a half feet long), snakes and tigers to worry about. Last July a man on patrol lost his right forearm to a tiger. Ugh!
Be sure and put 'B Btry' on my address.

Any food parcels at all will be welcome, especially canned things. How about some cashews?

That's about it for now. Say 'hi' to everyone for me and write soon.

Love,
   Me

§§§§§§§§§

I ponder that return address. I look at that way of addressing the envelope. Things are significantly different since just a few days before.

It is bizarre to think that while Donn was experiencing his first days in Vietnam, I was a college sophomore, acclimating to my new university. I was busy with college sophomore things.

I remember the TV filled with daily images of Vietnam, and I recall my confusion about some of the language used. I stumbled every day over the use of the word 'troops.' The news reported so many troops went into an area, so many were killed, so many were being sent over. I could not figure it out: Was a 'troop' a team unit? Was it an individual? I puzzled over it frequently, but I was far too embarrassed to ask anyone. It was obviously something I was supposed to know.

In 1966-67 I had been at the University of Wisconsin, where protests against the war were huge and widely publicized. At the time Donn was still being trained on American soil, and I was circumspect about everything related to war and protests. The lottery for the draft was on everyone's mind all the time. A few people had gone to Canada, but it didn't seem to be an option that many considered.

My memories of that year are a montage. The huge quad in front of Bascom Hall being turned into a cemetery, mock headstones as far as I could see as I made my way up that long hill to class.

A phone call in the middle of the night from a high school acquaintance—a very cute guy who was in a band in my hometown. He was obviously drunk and panicky, and he had called me to say he had gotten orders to go to Vietnam and he was scared. I had never talked with him personally before, and I never did after that. But that night I listened to the fear in his voice and heard him cry, over 2,000 miles of phone lines, to a girl he barely knew.

Someone had bombed a math building at Wisconsin. A graduate student was killed. It was, as I recall, a protest about UW's support of Dow Chemical, which made napalm. In 1985 I was living in Lake Jackson, Texas, married to a chemist who worked for Dow Chemical. Our son, Jeff, was a precocious toddler who said "Dow" as one of his first words. That's where his daddy worked. The company had worked very hard since the '60s to get people's minds off of napalm.

In the fall of 1967 I was on the campus of Duke University. Students were protesting there, too. There were sit-ins, an SDS chapter, the National Guard, and tear gas on campus occasionally. To say I was conflicted is an understatement. My brother had just gone to Vietnam.

On a walk across campus one day a gorgeous hippy asked me how I could stand it. How could I stand having my brother in Vietnam. I didn't know what to say. I looked at the guy and thought how I would love to date him. But I had no idea what to say to him about Vietnam or my brother.

When I took "American History from WWII to the Present," our professor assigned us a research paper. The topic was Vietnam: Research the beginnings of the conflict, analyze the build-up of American forces, and present a solution.

I threw myself into that project, even though history had never been my forte. But as I tried to find a solution after studying the background, I could not find one. There didn't seem to be a solution. There didn't seem to be any way for the war to end other than American withdrawal. It was 1967. No one in the US administration was talking about withdrawal. It seemed to me, the college sophomore, that we were in a no-win war and we would lose thousands of lives. It didn't occur to me that Donn would be one of them. I thought I would talk with him when he got home, get his opinion on possible solutions to the Vietnam conflict.

§§§§§§§§§

I took a few days off from this project to spend Labor Day with my family. College soccer games, some time at the mall with my daughter, some conversations with my husband and my son, and a lot of hours watching the beginning of the college football season and some of the matches of the US Open. I can feel my brother smiling his approval. He loved everything. He was going to be a cheerleader for Duke when he was there, but then he transferred to Roanoke College to be with Carolyn.

A male cheerleader?! Oh, yes, he explained to me. You should see how those guys get to hold the girls when they fall into their arms. And you should see the view…. I made him stop. Even at twelve years old, I got the gist of his desire to be a cheerleader.

In fact, when I was eleven and twelve years old, my brother had become my tutor in the ways of life. He gave me some steamy novels to read and told me to ask him if I had any questions. Sidney Sheldon's *The Other Side of Midnight* and a novel called *Boys and Girls Together* were his handbooks for teaching human sexuality. He shared with me "The Playboy Advisor." He gave me a copy of *Tropic of Cancer*, too, but I just couldn't go there.

When I was thirteen or fourteen, Donn presented me with a box of tampons. He said that I was to go in the bathroom, read the instructions, and not come out until I knew how to use them. No sister of his, he said, was going to wear pads.

In my pre-teen and early teen years, I watched from a distance the hilarity of my brother's high school life. He was a swinger, as he liked to say. He loved parties, he loved cars, he loved crazy hats. He had a big, flat hat that he called a pork-pie hat, and his smile when he wore that nutty thing could make anybody laugh. He and some friends formed a comedy troupe called The Splatters, and they performed all around Roanoke County. Donn loved comedy, and he bought record albums of the work of various comics, from Bill Cosby to Tom Lehrer. One of Donn's heroes was a new, young comic named Bob Newhart.

I read in the paper this morning that Bob Newhart is 75 years old today. Donn, on the other hand, is still 26.

Letter 6

Postmarked Sep 28, 1967.

Thurs Sept 28th

Toombie my Love,

Received your letter yesterday. Was very happy to hear from my fat ole mom; however, you better start slimming and get that hernia fixed, right? C'mon Toombie, don't procrastinate.

How did things go as the Nurse of GE? What a title! Glad to hear Dockie is happy at Duke.

Thanks for depositing the money---- do you know if that sum ($448.06) included the dividend from NY Life? How about any bills that may have come. What do I owe you? I wrote to "Time," "Playboy," and "Chicago Trib" and switched my address. If I fail to get them over here (magazines esp. "Playboy" are notorious for getting stolen) I'll switch them back to you. Time runs out in Jan '68 anyway. Yes, I did get my checks in Atlanta.

Give me a status report on the Marshmallow when you can. How about Runt Powell? Is he still working? He knows Porsches, I'm sure. Am concerned about the clutch.

Really enjoyed your joke about the aspirin.

Received a few letters from Kathy—guess her operation came out ok. Also had a letter from Boots in Germany—sounds like a good time over there.

Tomorrow we move to the Rockpile which is west of here. Probably be more action there.

So far I'm doing all right. I learn a little each day. The responsibility is tremendous here—we fire so much and there's always the chance we might goof and accidentally kill some of our own troops.

Right now I'm on duty from 2 AM to 2 PM. Currently it's 4:10 AM here.

About once a week we get the opportunity to go to communications headquarters and place a call to the states. I might give you a call someday. The way it works is this: via short wave radio we connect with an operator in San Mateo, Calif.; he, in turn, places a collect call to you. We can only speak for 3 minutes and after each time you speak you have to say, "Over." Got it? Well, I'm not sure when I'll try it, but at least you won't be too shocked to hear my voice if I do.

If you send a 'care' package please enclose some Scotch tape, Subdue shampoo and T.L.C.

Take care and give my love to Dockie.
Marquis De Sade

§§§§§§§§§

The opening paragraph of this letter makes me grin. "That's rich," as Donn used to say.

He refers to our mom as his "fat ole mom," tells her to start losing weight and get that hernia fixed. And he implores, "C'mon Toombie, don't procrastinate."

Let's see.....that was in 1967. Our mom was 56 at that time. She is now 95; she is definitely slimmer because she has shrunk with age. She lives with me in Atlanta about eight months out of the year, and she lives with my sister Joan in Connecticut in the summer months. In the last few years Mom has taken to commenting on how I have gained a bit of weight. And she NEVER got that hernia fixed! Ha!

Letter 7

Postmarked Sept 29, 1967. In Donn's writing, "Film Do Not X-ray" on mailing address side of envelope.

On other side of envelope, also in his hand, FILM Do NOT X-RAY! And P.S. Get SLIDES

Thursday

Toombie,

Here's my film—hope it gets there ok. Rush pictures back to me. I just sent a movie film in too. You should get that within 14 days. Do not send that back. Write me if you have any questions. If John G. says slides would come out better than pictures then get slides and send them to me along with a little viewer so I can see them.

That might be a better idea anyway. What do you think?

Love,
Donn
P.S. Let me know if this comes postage due.

Letter 8

Also postmarked Sept 29.

Fri 29 September

Toombie,

Sorry for the latest garbled letter. I decided I want slides instead of pictures (unless it can't be done) and do NOT send a viewer as I can get one here at the Marine PX ($1.90).

That's about it for now. I'm in charge of a convoy from Dong Ha to the Rockpile tomorrow. It will be a little tense, but nothing to worry about.

Please take care of your little lovable 'bod' and say 'hello' to John and MM and give a gentle kiss to the Marshmallow.

Luv,
Matt Brady

§§§§§§§§§§

Letters 7 and 8 give me a panicky feeling. I have no idea where the movies he shot are. I have no idea where all those slides or pictures might be.

Never the most organized person, I may have had custody of these at some point. I recall a black bag full of photographs or slides or movies or something, but all I can remember is lacking the courage to open it.

My cowardice.

I recall having an old movie projector in my mother's house in Roanoke years ago. When my father was alive, he was fascinated with the making of home movies. Some of my earliest memories from Schenectady are of my dad hauling out big umbrella-shaped lights so that he could shoot Christmas movies. And every Christmas Joan and Donn and I would dutifully come down the stairs while he filmed Christmas morning at the Sweet house. Later he would splice captions into the movies, a process which I could not fathom. I remember watching some of his home movies and miraculously there would be a frame that read "Snow at Christmas!" or "Galway Lake, 1951."

Donn also loved cameras and technology. He would make tape recordings and tape music from the radio onto his reels. Sometimes he would hide his gigantic tape recorder behind the sofa and just let it record whatever happened that particular, random day.

Sometimes I will find a reel of tape and wonder what in the world could be on it. It might be early work of

Diana Ross and the Supremes, or it might be a banal conversation among family members. One reel that I listened to about fifteen years ago had my dad's voice on it. He was lying in a rented hospital bed in his bedroom in our house in Roanoke, and he was sick with cancer. He was attempting to make jokes with some of the neighbors who had come to visit, and he was teasing my mom about being a mean nurse to him. The sound of his voice, that familiar Midwestern accent I hadn't heard since 1961, froze my heart and made my eyes go wide open and unblinking.

Letter 9

Postmarked October 12, 1967.
12 Oct

Hello Toombie girl,

Received your Oct 2 letter yesterday. I'm very confused about my finances. Can't understand why CB&T billed me $102.65 for one month. Enclosed are a couple of my finance papers that I'd like you to put in my tin box, ok? Do I still owe you money? Guess so—will send more later on.

Will you call Wheeler or whoever that was that sold me the life ins. and tell him that I want to change my use of the dividends on both policies. Instead of cash I want to apply the dividends against the premium. Thus my bill each year will be less and I won't have to fool with cashing a dividend check. Please call him and have him send me the necessary papers (if there are any). Thanx.

Glad to hear you're losing wt. Take care of yourself Toombs!
Just heard that Boston won game #6. Thru the Stars and Stripes newspaper we keep up fairly well with the ball scores.

How was your trip to Wnsboro and Richmond?
Glad to hear that the Marshmallow will get looked at.
It wasn't the gas cap that leaked—it was next to that,
where the fuel gauge fits into the tank. How about the
clutch?

So Tim F. joined the USMC.....hm-m-m. If he could
see these guys that just came to the Rockpile after 30
days at Con-Thien he might change his mind. I talked
to one today—said they lost 84 KIA's (killed in action)
and 942 wounded. Rough.

Today I take a convoy into Dong Ha and back. I don't
enjoy that—when the gooks ambush a convoy they
just about annihilate it. We've been lucky so far—hope
it continues.

I haven't felt too good for the last 5 days—GI upset.
Damn food.

Loved your latest Polock joke. Know why they only
give Polock factory workers a 10 minute break? If they
gave them 15 min. they'd have to retrain them.

Received a nice note from H & V. By the way, I've
lost Doc's address. What is it?

H & V said they got a "terrific picture" of my Porsche
at camp. Why don't you suggest they send me a copy
for Xmas. That'd be neatsy, yes? Said Howie's blood
press is now 120/75. Pretty good.

34

Dockie sent me a funny card in which she said, "When exactly do you get back to the states? I would like very much to know the exact date of your return as closely as you can figure, please."

Now why did she ask that? Don't tell her I wrote you this... but do you think she's planning on getting married or something? Hope you can shed some light on the mystery for me.

Well, that's about it for now. Have Wheeler take care of the ins please and write when you can.

LOVE,
Abdul Nasser

P.S. Sent in my application to U of Arizona Law School.

§§§§§§§§§

I suppose many of the letters are like this one. A composite of the mundane juxtaposed with bits and pieces of horror.

Donn had gone into the insurance business for about a year after he had finished some graduate work at the University of Virginia. His dream had been to go to medical school, but he had not gotten in right out of college. He then did some graduate work, took a job in New York as an independent insurance agent, and was drafted into the Army. He had decided to go to law school after the Army. While in New York, he saw a lot of our aunt and uncle, Howard and Viv, who had a camp at Galway Lake. Now that I have lived in the South for many decades, I would say they had a lake cottage. Before we moved south, our family used that family cottage every summer. It holds many memories, especially for my sister. One notable thing about that camp: Donn had had one of those small license plates made, the kind that you put on bicycles. His said "The Rock." He loved to think of himself as "The Rock," and he told me one summer that if I didn't call him "The Rock," he would not and could not answer me, because that was his name. He was in seventh or eighth grade at that time; I was in first or second grade. I watched with admiration as he nailed that license plate to the wall of the camp, where everyone would see that "The Rock" was there.

Acceptance letters to various law schools arrived at our house in Roanoke, and some arrived after he died. My mother would write "Killed in Vietnam" on the letters and return them to the schools.

I had forgotten that Tim F. had joined the Marine Corps. Tim was an acquaintance of ours. His parents were good friends with our mother. Tim killed himself playing Russian roulette with a loaded gun.

I expect Kurt Vonnegut to pop up anytime now and say "So it goes," or   Po-to-weet?

Letter 10

15 Oct.

Hello Sweet Toombie,

Yesterday I received your letter of October 7th and the CARE package with all the little goodies. Mom, please don't send packages air mail 1st class unless it's really necessary. It's too expensive. But I must say you do pack a fine care package. Loved the mini-poo especially.

So Tombo has TAS IV, oi wey! Glad to hear you had such a nice trip to W-boro and Richmond.

No, we don't wear stripes at the Rockpile—did you see where it is on the map in "Time" with Con Thien on the cover? Things are ominously peaceful here—we have gooks all around but not much contact.

Haven't been notified that I'm a 1st LT. yet, but the orders are usually late in getting here.

Did I tell you I got a package and letter from H & V? Sent me some cookies and cheese.

So far I've been real fortunate about mail. Usually get one or two letters a day. That really helps too!

You should have received the movies by now—how are they? When can I expect the slides? Be sure and package them carefully as after I look at them I'll send them back to you via Kathy probably.

The war continues over here. No one really knows who's where and what's going to happen, but I'm afraid something will soon.

It's been quite dry here the last three days. Getting cool in Roanoke now?

At any rate, take good care of yourself and if you get the new Playboy (Nov.), then put it in a small package or manila envelope and send it to me. If you just forward it in its own wrapper it will get "lost."
Give a kiss to the Marshmallow for me----

Love,
The Rock

P.S. If you should get any envelopes printed for me make sure they're the type that need no 'licking' to seal them. Why don't you just forget the whole idea? Too much trouble anyway.

§§§§§§§§§§

Have I already mentioned that Donn's middle name was Lafayette? Our dad's name was Alva Lafayette Sweet. The story goes that somehow the Sweet family could trace its Lafayettes all the way back to The Lafayette. Or maybe it was to someone who admired Lafayette. I have never investigated the genealogy. My sister has a great interest in it. I have always felt rather like an odd limb on the family tree.

Letter 10 comments on the birth of a child to one of Donn's best friends from high school. Our mom, who keeps in touch with everyone she has ever met, could tell you right now about Tom and his children and his grandchildren. A few years ago I drove Mom from Atlanta to Macon, GA, where Tom was hosting a birthday party for his mother. I hadn't seen Tom since he was a teenager.

The man in his sixties was camouflaging the boy I knew as Tom. I cannot imagine Donn in his sixties. I simply cannot.

Letter 11

Postmarked October 20, 1967.
19 Oct

Hello Toombie,

Received your letter of the 10th and card yesterday. It takes from 3 – 8 days for a letter to get here.

My base camp is Dong Ha and I get there about once a week or so. We got another LT into the btry (FO) and since we have to keep one officer in base camp at all times I may go to Dong Ha for a week or so since it will be my turn to go. Otherwise we stay in the field 90% of the time.

Would you look over my receipts and see if my allotments have been in effect since the last of Aug or the early part of Sept. I paid CB&T once by check (July) and Aug's payment was supposed to be sent by the Army. So, if you find 2 deposit slips (Sept and Oct) then I'm paid up and they overcharged me. If so, let me know and I'll write them. Give me the dates and figures.

Glad to hear the movies came out OK. I've been having trouble with my movie camera lately--- guess the humidity and grit are getting to it.

Haven't heard from Dockie in a while, how is she?

Give my regards to Stu B. Hope he's not suffering.

Had a funny letter from Ginny—Jinx broke his leg (caught in the garage door)- --she said Don was thinking of taking out Blue Cross for Jinx and Deacon.

Well lovable Toombie, take care of yourself and keep them cards and letters comin' in folks.

Love,
D. Lafayette

§§§§§§§§§

How strange it must have been. Witnessing killing and suffering in a war zone, yet having empathy for Stu, a friend of ours who was dying from cancer. The irony would not have been lost on Donn.

And yet he could laugh: Blue Cross for the dogs belonging to Ginny and Don, another aunt and uncle.

Both of our uncles fought in WW II, but neither of them ever said anything about it to anyone as far as I know. I didn't know until his funeral that my father-in-law had been in Patton's army. Is that how that generation dealt with surviving a war?

Letter 12

Envelope lost.

23 Oct

Hello Toombie,

Thanks for the letter—will enclose a check for the Playboy bill. Hope this about catches up my unpaid bills. Received a letter from Dockie yesterday—she's a riot. Too, I got a letter from Meigie J. Quite a surprise—nice of her to write. Today I had one from H & V. Love that mail!

Glad to hear you are losing weight—keep it up Mom!

Right now I'm on Kaopectate to fight diarrhea.

I received a form for an absentee ballot from the Rke County Repub. Committee—nice of them, but I'm going to abstain 'cause if I get into Ga. Law, then I'll want to qualify for in-state tuition.

I haven't heard about Patti Porsche's condition lately. How is she? What did Gino say about her? How much do I owe you for that? Is she sad for lack of T.L.C.?

I requested an R&R for Feb. My first choice is Bangkok, then Taipai (Formosa) and last is Australia.

Did I ever tell you I got the literature about law boards? I've written to Universities of: Chicago, Miami and Alabama for applications.

I'm in Dong Ha now. We have one gun here and I'm the only officer. We fire mostly at night. The battery will remain at the Rockpile for another 3-4 weeks probably. The war is about the same – worse if anything.

I sent another roll of movie film in –should get it in a couple of weeks. Most of the shots are from convoys between Dong Ha and the Rockpile. After you've seen them a couple times or whatever send them to H &V etc.

Received a curt note from Kathy—seems I don't write letters that match her affection for me. C'est la guerre. She's a nice girl but I'm waiting for a better looking one with money. 1st for love, 2nd for money (Old Toombie saying).

Well, luv, take good care of my favorite sister's mother and let me know what Hefner says.

Auf wiedersehen,
Guy

§§§§§§§§§

It is October in Vietnam, and Donn has diarrhea. He was always a small guy, so if he lost any more weight it must have been devastating.

Once when I was in high school I had a date with a very wealthy, handsome boy from the fancy part of town. It turned out that he was not a nice boy, and when I was trying to convince him to leave my house, I told him that my big brother would be home any minute. This might have been effective except that my brother did come home. And the not-nice boy was about five inches taller and 50 lbs heavier than my older brother. Fortunately, neither of them had any intention of confronting the other. Donn assured me afterward that he was "small but wiry, lean but mean." Tough to believe when he frequently had that big grin on his face.

One thing these letters are making clear: this young lieutenant was not Othello. Yes, he had loved his young wife dearly, he had fought to keep her, he had lost her to another man. But he was not depressed nor suicidal, even in the landscape that was Vietnam at war. To suggest that he died because he had not cared to live is romantic nonsense. I have no idea where that notion originated.

He had plans. An R&R in February. Law school. Finding another girl to share his life with. And yes, our mother had always said that the first time was for love, the second for money. She had only married once, and whether that was for love or for security is an open question. Our dad had been the romantic one.

I don't know why my sister married three times. I know that I married the first time because everyone – espccially my mother – thought I should marry this law student who had fallen in love with me. In fact, my psychiatrist would say, years later, that my mother should have married him. He had the perfect lineage, the perfect resume. The second time I married someone that I chose for myself. I am the balloon flying around in the air, and he is the guy holding the string. It has worked for 26 years and counting.

Letter 13

Postmarked October 27, 1967.
26 Oct

Hello Toombie,

Received your letter of the 20th today. Glad to hear the slides are in – am anxious to see how they turned out.

Yesterday I got a letter and package from Joan. She sent me some DELICIOUS brownies, think they're the best I ever tasted. I wrote her and thanked her for the package and asked Tony for something to combat my Vietnam syndrome . . . diarrhea. I've been taking KaoPectate and Paregoric but it hasn't helped yet.

Too bad Duke lost to Clemson – hope Doc had a good time anyway.

Joan said they would probably go to Rke for Thanksgiving or about that time in Nov.

If my Playboy mags are still being sent to 1948 Walmann then I'll leave it that way and you can send them to me whenever you have a package coming this way. My Time subscription runs out in Jan so that would make a nice Xmas gift if anyone inquires.

Evelyn Sweet-Hurd

How was the ice show at the coliseum?

Are you planning to work at all? What are your plans along that line? Too, what do you plan to do with the MG Midget? C'mon Toombie, let's be a little bit practical.

There isn't a great deal new here – we shoot and they shoot back. Same-same.

I hope you're feeling OK and that everything is going well for you. Do take care and thank you for writing so often.

Luv,
Son of Toombie

P.S. Did you go through John G. to get the slides?

§§§§§§§§§

The emphasis in the letters on keeping track of finances, on worrying about our mother's health, and the appeal – often underlined – to her to take care brings to my mind the last words Donn ever spoke to me:

"Take care of Mom."

Letter 14

Envelope lost.

27 Oct

Hello Lovable Toombie,

This afternoon I received your humorous Halloween card, beauty pix of Patti and note with very funny joke.

Patti looks lovely, guess the TLC is there even though I'm not. The only thing I especially look for in "care" packages is canned pears and peaches (small cans). Otherwise I really don't need too much. I could use some AG-1B flashbulbs for my camera. No flash cubes, just the little individual blue bulbs.

Pretty good about CSHS's football team—who's the coach now?

Not too much is new here. The convoy we sent to the Rockpile today was fired upon but I wasn't along. Nobody was hit.

Right now my diarrhea has subsided and I feel pretty good.

I received two long letters from Kathy yesterday and wrote her a curt reply. I feel guilty (somewhat) continuing the correspondence because I have no intentions of following them up when I return. And her letters are getting unrealistic.... As time passes she thinks I'm really something. You know, absence makes the heart grow fonder etc. Blah!

Once I'm able to start accumulating money instead of sending checks out I intend to get a complete stereo set up. Probably by June I ought to have some money saved up. Hope so.

Well, that's about all for now. Take care and STAY ON THAT DIET!

Luv,
Son of Toombie

§§§§§§§§§

Ah, CSHS. That's our old high school, Cave Spring High School.

I attended six years after Donn, but teachers recognized the last name and groaned when they discovered I was indeed his sister. Donn had been an unforgettable student.

When the CSHS concert band opened their music on stage to perform, the music had been rearranged.

Percussion had horn music, flutes had tuba music, saxophones had percussion music…. Donn had been busy on that stage before the curtains opened.

When the administration had strictly informed the students that no one was to go into another person's locker, for whatever reason, the next morning Kotex pads spilled out from all the lockers as they were opened before homeroom.

One of the stuffiest English teachers on earth entered her classroom to find the movie screen had been lowered over her chalk board. She huffily raised it up to find a Playmate of the Month taped to her board.

The Donn years at CSHS had resulted in the creation of a demerit system for students.

After Donn's funeral, my mother thought it would be appropriate to give the ceremonial flag to CSHS. And I have heard that there is a plaque somewhere in the building that lists the alumni of CSHS who died in Vietnam. I realize that students in those hallways today have no hint of the personalities of the people on that list. They would have loved Donn. He was fun.

Letter 15

Postmarked October 31, 1967.

Monday, 30 Oct

Hi Toombie,

Enclosed is my pay voucher for Oct and a letter from the Great Howe. Thought you'd enjoy it. Put both in my tin box, ta-ta. Notice that Howard's letter is without stamp and came postage due. But, they never try and collect from us so why don't you try it. Write the same thing he did and give it a whirl.

This coming Thurs or Fri I'm being sent to the ARVN airborne (Army Republic of Viet Nam) unit as an F. O. I don't know how long I'll be out there – probably two weeks or so. Anyway I can't send any mail (or receive any) so don't worry if you don't hear from me for awhile. Before I leave, though, I'm going to finish up my current role of film and send it to you.

This ARVN unit is operating right on the DMZ and usually along the coast. Hope all is peaceful while I'm with them.

Well, take care and I'll write again before I leave.

Love,
Donn

§§§§§§§§§

These references to his tin box are driving me crazy. I need to ask our mother about it.

The tone of this letter turns somber when he talks about going out as a Forward Observer. And he writes the word "Love," and he signs his name "Donn."

When I was in graduate school at Baylor in the 1980s I taught freshman English. Often our textbooks would have a selection referencing Vietnam. I never included that selection, as I couldn't trust myself to stay steady on my feet if I tried to teach it. But one semester I decided to include another selection about another war. In the course of the class discussion, a young man stated that American wars since WWII were for the underclass to fight. He went on to say that no college graduates, no middle or upper-middle class white soldiers became "cannon fodder" as Forward Observers in Vietnam.

Cannon fodder.

Letter 16

Postmarked Nov 2, 1967.

1 Nov

Lovable Toombie,

Got your Oct 25th letter last nite. I just wrote a letter to
CB&T about my loan—I'm still confused. I thought
before I left Rke in Sept that a statement came from
the bank or the Army saying I was credited for 102.65
for Sept. Guess not, eh? At any rate get out my 2 NY
life policies and send them postage due to: Mr. James
D. Yancey, CB&T Co, P.O. Box 120, Columbus,Ga.
31902. Do this after you've talked to Wheeler about
changing my dividend from cash to reduction of
premium. (He might need to see the policy).
Ta-ta.

Glad to hear you're pampering Patti. Am looking
forward to Jean Pritchard's care package. Ginny said
she was going to send one but I never got it.

I just saw the latest issue of Playboy and now I know
where your supply of jokes comes from. Toombie =
sneaky.

Evelyn Sweet-Hurd

I got the package with slides. Very disappointing—so small. I'll send them back before too long and I want you to try them in a regular slide projector and see how big they come out. Too, please rush me some black and white film for the Minox (cassette type). I'm going to get snapshots made from now on I guess…. Color is horribly expensive. Oh well, such is life.

Well, that's it for now—

Toodle and Luv,
Fearless Son-of-Toombie

Letter 17

Envelope has no postmark.

5 Nov

Hello there,

Yesterday I arrived here at hill #23. We left Dong Ha at 0700 in a driving rainstorm and took a boat up the river to the coast and a Marine camp called Qua Viet. The day before, Qua Viet had been shelled and a dentist and 3 others were killed. From Qua Viet we got on a USMC Amtrack which is a large, tracked vehicle that is also amphibious. I have 2 spec 4's with me....DeLano and Riutta. After a long hot (I got burned on my arms) ride we arrived at hill #23. The rain stopped at Qua Viet and the sun came out; the country from Qua Viet up to here and beyond is all sand dunes and it is hot. On the trip up here we had to go at a snail's pace because we were sweeping the road for mines (found 7).

Hill 23 is currently held by 1st BN ARVN Airborne. There are 5 Americans here. My team (3) and a Marine (who directs naval gun fire) and the advisor to the ARVNs. . . Maj. Duckworth.

We have C-Rations to eat. Our water is obtained from the crick that runs thru our camp – we add Iodine tablets to make it potable. For a latrine we use a shovel to dig a hole. Lovely. About a 10 minute walk from here is a swimming hole where we can bathe. It's about waist deep.

To the north of us is hill 31. Bad news.

7 Nov.

Just learned that there will be a helicopter up here soon to pick up some mail etc… So….

Yesterday was very exciting – we found 120 Russian made 152 rockets buried about 1000 meters NE of here. Today we are supposed to have an Amtrack come get them. This was a very important find. The rockets were to be used on Dong Ha. They are big and heavy. Then, last nite an ambush the ARVNs had worked and they killed 2 VC and captured 2 automatic weapons (AK-47's). I took pictures of the rockets and one of the dead VC. (He was 28 and was from GioLinh—or so his papers said.)

I sleep (?) in a hammock which isn't too satisfactory, but it prevents the centipedes from getting to me. My bunker is about 4 x 7 and about 5' tall. I walk in a crouch now.

I sent DeLano up to hill 31 where he can see well what's to the north. They receive a lot of incoming arty there and it's nervewracking I hear. I will relieve him soon.

Well, that's about it for now. I hope this letter gets thru. Happy BD to Dockie and hello to everyone who reads this.

Take care,
Donn

P.S. I can now count in Vietnamese and ask for a "Playgirl" – may be nice to know some day—yes?
P.P.S. Yesterday an Amtrack hit a mine 3 kilos south, 2 wounded.

§§§§§§§§§

I have only seen war in the movies. And I haven't even watched some of the more graphic movies. So I think it is fair to say that I haven't any idea of what the conditions of war have been for any soldier, anywhere.

In Piedmont Park in Atlanta this week they have set up a refugee camp. The Doctors Without Borders set it up, in an attempt to help the rest of us see what living in a refugee camp looks like, feels like. I doubt that they attempted to simulate the smell.

It is difficult for me to read that Donn took pictures of the dead VC. Twenty-eight years old. I wonder if anyone took a picture of Donn after his throat was severed by shrapnel?

If this book finds publication, I am sure one of the sentences in letter 17 will take on new meaning:

"Hello to everyone who reads this."

Letter 18

No postmark.

14 Nov

Dear Toombie, Dockie, Joanie, Tony, Suzanne and Patti,

Received my first mail since I got here yesterday and so I'll start a combined reply of your letters (Toombie's of 27 and 30th Oct and Joan's of 29th Oct).

I am now on Hill 31 east of Gio Linh. From this large, windswept sand dune I can see the ocean to the east and well into North Vietnam to my north across the Ben Hai River. Three days ago it started raining and it hasn't stopped since. I guess this is the monsoon at last. I am absolutely miserable as far as personal comforts go. We are always damp if not wet. Am living in bunkers that leak. Words fail me when I try to describe life here. We have no latrine so it's squat over a hole in the rain-- The ARVNs have a latrine but it's nauseating, the floor is covered with maggots. I prefer to get wet than endure that. Diarrhea becomes a real problem here. Tony suggested I see the medics for pills, I suggest the Army send us a medic. On this particular outpost is a company of ARVNs, 5 Marines (for adjusting naval gunfire) and Donny-poo. My two corporals are now on Hill 23 about 1000 meters to the south.

So far we have had moderate contact with the enemy. Four nites ago in a short fire fight we lost nine men (4 dead and 5 wounded) and killed about 13 NVA. We captured 3 weapons. It's really a helluvan existence. C'est la guerre.

Toombie, I was in Dong Ha before coming up here, not Da Nang. Da Nang is a paradise compared to Dong Ha not to mention this soggy hill. Hope Dockie liked the BD present—send me a pix of you with the bikini pants, Doc.

Hope J & T got the slides. Right now I'm using B &W film and will get snapshots printed. Plan now to get a good 35 mm camera. If my B & W pictures come out I'll have shots of a dead VC, captured weapons, etc. I wonder if Life magazine knows I'm up here. For a while I was eating with the ARVNs but got tired of rice and unknown side dishes. Chop sticks were a pain anyway.

Heard on the radio last night that Duke beat Navy-- Bon.

I got the craziest letter from John G. – will answer it when I get back to Dong Ha in 15 days or so.

Received a nice letter from Charlie S. – He's in his last year at U of Ga Law. Good ole Chas, what a great Heeb.

Joan, I enjoyed your jokes; glad to see that you're keeping busy at Lockheed. Yuk.

Do you know what they call it when the Polish paratroopers jump? Air pollution. What happens when you cross a chicken with an elephant?

You get a dead chicken with 12 inch ass hole.

Well enough of that.

Some of my envelopes are sealed before I get them so I slit them open and tape them shut. No censorship of mail that I know of.

I'm sitting on a wet sand bag in my rain suit writing this by candle light. I eat all my meals (C-Rations) by candle light. Ain't that romantic? Loverly.

That's about all I can think of now—as a matter of fact I'm not too sure I can even think any more.

In your next package, care-type, I'd like some TLC, vitamin tabs, an up-to-date status report on Patti, mail from beautiful women, food, soup, booze, and a picture of Snoopy.

Evelyn Sweet-Hurd

Well, now I'm getting cold and stiff so I guess I'll go peer thru my binos and see if I see anything to shoot. Right now the battery that fires for me is a Marine 155 mm outfit at Gio Linh.
Take care kin folk,

Peace in our time,
N. Chamberlain

Letter 19

No postmark.
17 Nov

Dear Mother of the Son of Toombie,

Received beaucoup mail today, will start to reply by writing to you. Impressed?

Enclosed is a letter from CB&T and check. Please deposit check and put letter and bottom of check in my tin box. When I get back I'll try to straighten that mess out.

Have not received any package from Ginny yet will let you know when I get it. You won't believe this but I did get a package from H & V…. in it I found tin cans of goodies and a plastic bag with a black oblong soft smelley object. At first I thought it was a squashed chocolate éclair, the Marine captain living with me thought it was a piece of liver. You know what we figured it was? A BANANA!!! What would make someone think a banana would make it to Vietnam in edible condition? Oh, well, it was funny—will write them a thank you note. This smearing is where I just smacked a mosquito – he or it was full of blood apparently. Goddamn they're nasty tonite.

I will write David S. a letter before too long. Would you send me his address? Sorry to hear he's with another church.

Hope everything went well Thanksgiving with the family. Joan gave me a subscription to the Atlanta Constitution for Xmas and I've already received 4 copies. Really nice of her. I got 1 letter from Joan and 2 from Doc today as well as 2 law school apps and several letters from Kathy. Too, got a real nice letter from Cindy E., really funny. Your funny card was a riot. The real Toombie, yes? Yuk.

Give my regards to Stu—sure hope he doesn't suffer too much. Tell him I welcome any good jokes.

The M-16 is a good weapon—has to be kept clean that's all. The AK-47 is a Chicom rifle that is better than our M-16 but it's a little heavier and of course that's just my opinion.

The cartoons were very amusing. Ta-ta. Mom, the 1st Inf Division is near Saigon. I'm on the DMZ with the Marines. Look for the names Gio Linh and Dong Ha.

How did my movies turn out?

As you know I'm still out here in the boonies and will be here for probably another couple weeks. I don't mind at all. No one bothers me and as long as I can stay reasonably dry and we don't get attacked I'm OK. This is a pretty good position (as long as we don't have to defend it) as we can see a good ways and shoot all over the place. If we get hit, though, it's going to be hairy.

If you ever meet someone connected with the Roanoke Times or World News ask them if they'd like me to write a short column for them. Sort of an eyewitness account. I can always use some extra cash. Just a wild thought.

Listen Toombie. I want you to please do the following and write me on what you do and the results etc. Please have the valves on my Porsche set for the proper setting (about a 20 min procedure) and have my oil changed correctly. I want the filter screen cleaned etc. The manual explains how it should be done. I don't want them to simply drain the oil out the plug and put some new oil in. Check it out and have it done right. The valves should be checked monthly. Also the tires should be checked for proper pressure. One of them loses pressure over a couple weeks time.

Please take care and let me know what the story is and how much I owe you.

Thanks Mom.

Luv,
Patti's Lover

P.S. How's the clutch?

Letter 20

No postmark. Thanksgiving Day

Happy T.D. Toombie,

How are things with my #1 mother? How did you celebrate the holidays? How's Patti? Are you getting those things done?

Wrote a letter to David S. – please forward. I got a batch of mail 2 days ago which included letters from Billy E., you, H&V and Kathy. Kathy said she's sent me a Xmas tree, pretty nice eh? Did I tell Cindy E. also wrote me?

Hill #31 (my present location) is a busy little place lately. For the last 2 days we've been shelled with astounding accuracy. We had 4 shells land within a 50ft. radius of our bunker – scared the hell out of me as the bunkers just slow down these shells and don't actually stop them. Then the nite before last we had a small ground attack. We had 2 wounded while we killed 4 NVA. Early the next morning we went out hunting and I found one of the dead NVA – took his belt off of him and thereby got a dandy souvenir. If my pictures come out you'll see it. Anyway it's all very exciting and I'll be glad to leave. Speaking of that –

still don't know how much longer I'll be up here.

The enclosed pix is taken from our battery at Dong Ha. Really blackened the sky that day.

Mom, it's now 2 hours after I wrote the previous sentence, just as I finished writing 'day' we were hit by NVA artillery. We took 13 rounds and had 1 killed and 3 wounded. I have been directing counter battery artillery but their guns are about 10,000 meters north of here in NVN and it's hard as hell to spot them while the rounds are coming in. At any rate I'm still alive and kicking. Hooray for our side! Be sure and show Stu the picture and tell him if he'd stop demonstrating against the war, then he can use the enclosed coupon to gain free access to our side.

Well, lovable Toombie, I don't know when this letter will ever get out of here, but at least you know I still love you and Patti. Please take care and let me know what Hefner told you.

Au revoir,
Fearless Son of Toombie

P.S. At this location we have:
   2 companies ARVN
   4 US Marines
   1 Australian
   3 US Army
Quite the international group.

§§§§§§§§§

This morning I was reading over what I had written so far, searching for typos, wondering about my commentary. I found two typos, and I sat at my desk again to begin work. But I felt a little greasy, and I had to make a decision: get started or take a shower first.

The absurdity nearly drowns my voice. The conditions in which Donn was trying to live and the choices I have to make today in my life are from different parts of a truly absurd universe. Centipedes, maggots, dysentery, corpses. Take a shower now in my new home, which has a ridiculously large master bathroom, or later. Recycle the Dial shower gel container, or throw it in the trash. Get a snack now or wait until a bit later. Answer my cell phone or let it take a message.

Cell phone! Donn would be excited about the technology.

Some decades ago I spent too much time studying Theatre of the Absurd. The problem, I came to realize, was that I didn't need to study it. It made perfect sense to me. Other members of my class were exclaiming about this and that, and I was just like a duck in water.

A few weeks ago I saw a BBC interview of Nick and George Clooney. George Clooney is a world famous movie star, and his dad Nick is a journalist. I had never heard of Nick, surprise surprise. That's the way our world works. Anyway, George and Nick Clooney were trying to get people to notice that there is genocide going on in Darfur. Nick said that George had decided to use his "celebrity card" to bring attention to the matter. A perfectly good use of celebrity, I think. People in America are too busy right now to notice Darfur. We have the new fall season of TV shows, we have mid-term elections, we even have Iraq and Afghanistan if we want to go into dark and scary places.

Bob Woodward has just published a new book about the denial taking place in our administration regarding Iraq.

When I was younger I never really believed the cliché that history repeats itself.

When the BBC interviewer was beginning her interview with George and Nick Clooney, she introduced them as Mr. and Mrs. Clooney. She then quickly tried to correct that, but then she said Mrs. and Mr. Clooney. Somehow she managed to go to the first question while father Clooney and son Clooney were laughing. Don't you just know that if that interviewer could have one "Do Over" in her career, that would be it?

I look back and think about my own journey and those of my brother. I have made lots of mistakes that I would like to take back. Donn made lots of choices, and I had no influence over any of them. But if I could have one Do Over for both of us, this would be it:

Canada.

Letter 21

Postmarked Dec 2, 1967.

30 Nov

Hello Toombie,

Well, I'm back in Dong Ha now. The battery is still at the Rockpile so I'll probably be going out there again soon. When I got back yesterday I had about 10 packages and 15 letters waiting for me. Some of the food parcels were spoiled—c'est la guerre. I received packages from Kathy, H & V, Goldstock, Jean P., Joan and You. Your food, film and fruit came thru OK.
Ta-ta.

I'm enclosing my pay vouchers for my files. Say, can you tell me what my last bank statement read? How much do I have now?

Received a nice letter from Pris-- after I answer it I'll send it on. She went ahead and divorced Bill and then Bill and Carolyn promptly married. In a way it was kind of a shock to learn that little ole Carowinnie is now a Mrs. again. Ah me. I'm lucky I got out the way I did. Next time I'll have to get a girl with nice parents.

Thanx for taking care of the life ins policies. Did you get the movies straightened out. I think your problem was with the projector, was it?

Never did get a package from Ginny although I got a letter from her – maybe the package will come yet.

Your T---g card via the "Great Howe Trick" came thru OK. 'Free' and postage due. P.S. Joke.

All through with the Pick kids? Sounds like you enjoyed it.

Too bad about Stu—hope he doesn't suffer. Keep me posted. The brownie troop project of "boxes for soldiers" sounds great. Hope they come thru with them.

Glad to hear you're still winning bridge prizes. I knew Joan got her talent somewhere.

No, I have never received a note from the Zirks. Probably waiting for Xmas.

Mucho-mucho gracias for writing so often. You're one in a million, Toombie. Ta-ta.

Toombs, your jokes just slay me. Some are SO bad (snicker) and others are really funny. Ta-ta.

Hope that J & T & S got to Roanoke OK. Good to hear

Dockie is well and happy – what a great kid she is.

Amazing that VMI beat VPI.

Nice of Mrs. Smothers to give you the invitation.

The weather here is now cold and raining like hell—
B-R-R.

Received another funny letter from Goldstock. He and
Howie both sent me knives – won't tell them that,
natch. Anyway, it struck me funny.

Kathy sent me a Xmas tree which is about 4 feet tall
and really nice. Poor girl, she really likes me – don't
mean to sound conceited. Just the facts ma'am.

I'm sitting on my bunk writing this—that's why it isn't
too neat.

Well, Love, will stop for now.

Will write again soon when my back isn't so sore.

Take care Marion,
SOT

Son of Toombie

§§§§§§§§§

Letter 21 gives me pause. When Donn says he "received a nice letter from Pris" and that "Bill and Carolyn promptly married" I have to consider how much to go into all of that.

I think it is enough here to say that "little ole Carowinnie," the sunshine in Donn's life when she was his wife, left Donn to be with Bill, a physician who was married and had four children and one more on the way. Pris is the wife who was left behind, the mother of the four and soon to be five children. Pris and Donn had become friends in their misery as the affair between Dr. Bill and Nurse Carolyn killed the marriages. The Carolyn story continued to be a fascinating one, and I kept up with it for a while.

In fact, years after Donn's death I reconnected with Carolyn, who was at the time living just about an hour from me. She convinced me that we could revive our friendship, and I actually went to visit her and Bill. It was like an out-of-body experience. I recall recognizing that this was indeed Carolyn, and here she was with this man she called her husband, and they had Dalmatians and a boat.

A few years later Bill left Carolyn for a lab tech in his hospital.

Carolyn then went through a wild-eyed Jesus Freak stage; she came to visit me, literally thumping a Bible.

She started anew at a different hospital, she contracted hepatitis, she married a very young man. I think she was 30 or 31 and he was about 22. That marriage was eventually annulled.

The last thing I heard from her was when she called me in Texas to say that she had discovered, finally, what she needed, and that her new partner, her soul mate, was a woman named Peggy.
I couldn't make this stuff up.
I wonder what Donn would have said about any of that.

Letter 22

Postmarked Dec 5, 1967.
4 Dec

Hello Lovable Toombie,

Tonite I'm going to try and call you – hope it goes thru OK.

Just a note to let you know a few things—

Many thanx for the photo of the family.

Received a nice card from the Zirks.

Ginny said she's sent me 3 packages—must be on a slow boat.

Had my friend Bob Reich take some Polaroids of me 'cause I needed some for law school apps. How do I look? Like Dad?

Wrote a thank you note to Jean P.

Sent Ernie B. a character reference form for law school – told him he'd be un-American unless he gave me a good reference.

Kathy continues to write and send me food – think she's desperate.

Put Howe's letter in my tin box.

I leave the 7th for Gio Linh – will FO from the towers there. I'll probably do that until mid-Jan.

After Wed I'll have 4 law applications pending—Ga, Arizona, Stetson (Fla) and McGeorge in Sacramento, Calif.

Must write letters to H & V, Boots, Pris and Ginny, plus Joan and Doc.

I've been busy with these law applications.

It's still cold and raining here – muddy.

What about your health status?

What about Patti's health?

Still having problems with diarrhea – my tail's sore. Can't get pills here – all out. Have been for two and a half months. Guess I'll write Don E. for some.

Please take care,
Donn-e-poo

Letter 23

Postmarked Dec 9, 1967. On the flap of the envelope is a sticker. It has a drawing of Snoopy sitting on his doghouse. Snoopy is giving Woodstock, whose nest is on the doghouse, a kiss, and there are two little hearts. The roof of the doghouse has this on it, in red letters:
SEALED WITH A KISS
7 Dec

Hullo Mumzy,

Guess you figured out we couldn't get thru to the US with the phone call. Well, I'll try again someday. We leave tomorrow for Gio Linh.

Received your letters of 29 Nov and 2 Dec. Enjoyed the Xmas card. (I'll be your Valentine).

I received your package—it was great! You sent many of the things that I really need. The soup will really be welcome, as well as the nuts, Snoopy, fruit, etc. You pack a very fine care package. I also received a can full of homemade vanilla caramel from Pris – really good.

Wrote what I thought was a funny letter to Ant Virginny – she said she's sent 3 packages—haven't received any yet.

Say, when will you go to work? What about Hefner? Patti? Your plans for Xmas? Etc.

Now, please send my Playboys to me in your packages. I don't mind you stealing their jokes but I would like to see them, OK? (What did you think about the interview with Johnny Carson in Dec). Anyway, please send. Are you still getting my Time magazines? I'm not. Do NOT just forward the Playboys.

Oh, guess what? Received a Xmas card and letter from Judy Moleski – the name really threw me – that's H & V's Judy.

If you see the book <u>The Exhibitionists</u> do send. Hear it's kind of like <u>Valley of the Dolls.</u>

It's raining like hell here – mud everywhere.

Did you ever send my movies on to Ginny and H & V?

Well lovable Toombie, please take care of yourself and Snoopy and Donniepoo thank you.

Toodle
S.O.T.

§§§§§§§§§

This pile of letters from Donn is interrupted by a letter addressed to Mr. Donald Sweet from The University of Arizona College of Law. Business postmark of 5 cents.

Postmarked Dec 11, 1967, from Tuscon, Ariz.

On the envelope is a note in my mother's handwriting:

Sat – Dec 16

Wrote to you this AM – but this came this PM – thought you'd like to see it. Also got your letter of Dec 7. More another day—In haste Mom.

§§§§§§§§§

Here is the letter, typed on University of Arizona College of Law stationery:

December 11, 1967
Dear Mr. Sweet:

I am pleased to inform you that you have been admitted as a member of our September, 1968, first-year class.

You will be receiving an official certificate of admission from the Director of Admissions of The University of Arizona in the near future.

Evelyn Sweet-Hurd

We are looking forward to your being a member of our student body next year.

Sincerely yours,

John J. Irwin, Jr.
Assistant Dean

§§§§§§§§§

The acceptance letter is addressed to Mr. Donald Sweet. I wonder if Donn had applied as Mr. Sweet rather than as Lieutenant Sweet.

In any case, it was not unusual for people to assume his name was Donald.

It wasn't.

His name was Donn.

Letter 24

Postmarked Dec 15.

12 Dec

Hello Toombie,

Well, I'm now at Gio Linh. It is unbelievable! The mud is fantastic – with all this rain it's no wonder but it's still hard to believe. Everything gets stuck – wheeled vehicles are out of the question – bulldozers have trouble. Anyway I'm filthy and stay wet and muddy. I work from sunrise to early afternoon as an FO in a 50 foot tower. When we can see (the rain lets up once in awhile) then we can usually spot some NVA and then we shoot. It's all very exciting and not too dangerous. The worst part is the mud and the general living conditions – I share a very muddy bunker with 2 other guys and several rats. The rats here are ENORMOUS – if I kill one I'll send you its picture.

I've received food packages from all 3 aunts and uncles (H & V, Ervins and Zirks) plus one or 2 from Kathy. I also received a cute letter from Cindy – it sure is nice to have thoughtful relatives.

Mom, I never thought I could live in such dirt. My hands never are clean and I probably consume as much dirt and mud as I do food.

So far I'm doing fine though – I'm eating fairly well, taking my vitamins and antimalarial pills and killing people and H2O buffalo. To direct artillery fire on the enemy is such an impersonal way to kill. Sure wish we could go in after them and really wipe them out.

How are you doing? How's lovable Doc? When does she get home? What's new with Patti?

Want you to know the Campbell's soup is really a life saver – it's cold here and the hot soup is 'veddy' nice.

Please take care of yourself and give my best to Bobbie and Stu.

Merry Xmas,
"X"

P.S. Hope you'll send me the Jan. Playboy.

Letter 25

Postmarked Dec 17, 1967.

Addressed to Toombie and Dockie Sweet at our home address.

15 Dec

Hi there Dockie,

How is my beloved sister? I received your neatzy-keen, super cool book on Snoop's philos. Naturlich, it was – is great and I refer to it often.

Good to hear that Thanksgiving vacation was a success – hope Xmas turns out even better.

How are things at D.U.? Will you go into exams with a good average? Hope you do OK. Sorry to hear about your 2 "hang-ups," but they don't sound too serious – the Great Analyst has speaked, er, spoken. Anywho, I immensely enjoyed and appreciated your missive and look forward to more.

So how's my #1 Toombie? Did she go to Hefner? What did he say? She won't tell me so I'm counting on you. She also avoids: mentioning work, money, preventive maintenance on Patti--- oil change, valve clearance adjusted, tire pressure, TPR (temp, pulse, respiration). Help!

Right now I'm at Gio Linh, or right about here. (Arrow to map, which is in left bottom corner of this stationery).

The mud here is unbelievable – I hope my pictures come out OK so you can appreciate how the machinery of war comes to a squashing (sp) halt. Thank god for helicopters.

I'm sharing a bunker with a guy named Chimielewski (Irish?) who is my buddy over here. He's funny as hell and we get along fabulously considering he's 50% Polish and 50% Hungarian and Catholic. Anyway we've got the best equipped and most comfortable hooch on this hill. We've also killed 9 rats since moving in and we've seen one more – and so it goes. Kill people and kill rats. Loverly.

Starting tomorrow I'll go back to Dong Ha for 2 days and then come back up here for 4 -6 days and so on. At least that way I'll get to clean up once a week or so.

As you know I've got 4 applications pending for law school – sure hope something comes through. It will be nice to have my future decided for me concerning the next few years. Oh well, that's a long way off—or so it seems now from this place.

How's Duke doing in B-ball?

What are you going to major in? What courses will you take spring semester?

Well, luv, merry Xmas etc and my best to my favorite girls and please write soon.

Toods,
Donn-e-poo

Hi Mummy,

Just wanted you to know that I mitch you and LUUV you beaucoup. Keep me posted and have a happy….
Take care of Dockie for me and give Patti some Amoco unleaded for me.

With much love,
Son of Toombie

P.S. Expect Xmas presents around March.

Letter 26

Postmarked Dec. 18, 1967.
17 Dec

Hello Toombs,

I'm furious with myself because I've lost your last letter—when I got it I was in a rush and hastily read it and then who knows what I did with it?

I remember that you asked about a Sears bill—yes, I wrote them for some socks—please pay the bill. That's about all I remember—please send my bank balance again as I forgot that figure too. Damn is this ever annoying!

In the last few days I've received: 4 packages--- Dot Morack (send me her address so I can thank her), Mrs Bowers, Ginny (mailed the 11th of Oct) and Boots. Boots sent me a cute little bottle cork from Munich. Dot and Ginny sent me some excellent goodies. Love to get booze – especially scotch and good ole Ant Virginny always comes thru for me. Mrs Bowers package was nice but I doubt if I'll be able to get many guys to write T-you notes. After all, a package of gum etc is nice but . . . Anyway I'll write her in "behalf of the troops."

Too bad that Stu is being such an ass – well, self pity is a terrible thing and can destroy weak people.

Later—

Damn, damn, damn. Just got my minox B&W shots back and only 40% came out and those poorly at that. They said I had defective film. If the pictures I have in there now don't come out OK I'm ready to junk it. Speaking of cameras I just bought another one – this is a 35 mm—similar to Tony's but not as good or expensive. It's nice and I hope it works better than the Yashica. I bought a Canon FT QL. It's an SLR with thru the lens meter. I imagine that didn't make any sense to you. Ask John G. how lousy a choice I made – our selections are extremely limited up here. Mine has a 50 mm 1.8 lens – all for <u>only</u> $99. GULP!

Received a Xmas note from Bobbie Bensel. Also got a 7 page letter from Myrna on perfumed stationery which is so smelly I had to take it outside to read it. Guess I'll send it on to you. Doubt if I'll answer her as I don't really need another pen pal – I just get tired of writing letters. As it is I carry on a running correspondence with about a dozen people.

I guess I'm just tired and coming down with a cold.

By the way did you ever get Patti's gas leakage or seepage fixed? What about the clutch? Why don't you answer my questions about her?

Is she being unfaithful too? GROWL.

Well, must go out and check up on things.

Take care and the next letter is bound to be more cheerful.

Love to you'ns,
SOT

P.S. Started getting my Time magazines and also thank Mrs Swain for the Xmas card she sent me.

Letter 27

Postmarked Dec 22, 1967

19 Dec

Hi There Toombie and Dockie (if you're still home),

How are my goils today? Today has been beautiful (weather-wise) and good ole Gio Linh isn't too muddy lately.

My health went to hell these last few days and I'm treating myself with penicillin pills that I had stashed away and/but I feel better tonite. Dirty, sore throat and my face is broken out but other than that (and my hair lip) I'm beauty personified.

Hope the shower for Marcia and the wedding come off OK.

Pretty funny about Audrey F. – let me know where Tim finally ends up over here, if he's this far north I could probably see him some time.

How did the brochure of U of Arizona look? I wonder where I'll be this time next year....

Evelyn Sweet-Hurd

Glad that Jean P. enjoyed my note—ironic, because her package was spoiled when I got it—of course, I didn't tell her that.

Can't understand why you can't find Gio Linh on the map – it's about the only village of any size on the DMZ.

I've received 2 or 3 of Ginny's packages now—also got one from you today. Many thanx for the really outstanding gifts—without doubt they are KEEN. The cards were cute too—especially the one which reads "With you away in the military…" I enjoyed that one because I received the same card from H&V and the Ervins.

I think I'll be moved to another job before long. The colonel here told me that Cpt. Kruse has requested that I be his XO (executive officer) so I'll probably move in a few weeks.

As XO I'd be primarily concerned with ammo supply – guess it will be a nice change. Time will tell.

Received a funny letter from Charlie Swartz. He said Eric Heiner's brother, Phil, is now teaching a class at Ga. Law School. Chas graduates this year ('68) and then will either go into the Air Force or the Coast Guard.

Sure hope this cold goes away ASAP so I can be happy.

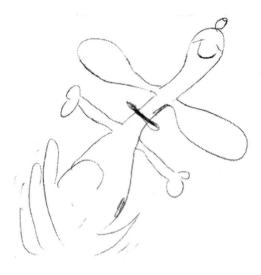

Well, that's about it for now. Please take care and hope your Xmas was loverly and the New Year fun-zee.

Toodle for now

's

Dear Hearts

SOT

Letter 28

Postmarked Dec 27, 1967.
28 Dec

Dearly Beloved Toombie,

Have received many gifts and letters since writing you last. I was greatly surprised to receive a package and card from Mrs. Deer (Dr. Edmunds' office nurse), and also packages from Mrs. Smothers, Dot Morack and Hope Stone. Had cards from the Montagues, Ballous, Bob Dyer, Batemans, Pritchards and the enclosed letter from Dean Sutton. How do you like dem apples? Please tell Jean P. I enjoyed her card. I'll write a short thank you note to Mrs Bowers later tonite. Hope to get at least one other guy to write too.

I was mighty happy to read U of Arizona's letter of acceptance. How come you haven't mentioned it in your letters? I still want Ga., as it's cheaper, but at least my future is decided – I guess.

I've been quite sick lately but after much sleep and pills etc I'm back on my feet.

I am now the XO of Service Battery and I think I will like it fine. I won't have to move around now as far as personal items are concerned and I have more freedom and responsibility. Anyway it's a change of pace.

Glad that Stu's a little better and that he got Bobbi something.

How was TAS III and TAS IV? Must write Mrs Smothers a letter thanking her for the goodies. People certainly have been nice to me – must be Toombie's influence, yes? I also received another Ant Virginny package.

I did reply to John G's letter, did he get it? Does MM still love me?

Hope Doc got in OK and everything went smoothly at the wedding. Love that Dockie.

I'd love some pfeffeneusse—H&V sent me some and it was great. Since I'm not in the "boonies" any more (at least for awhile) don't send any more soup but I can always use fruit, nuts, Scotch, cookies, etc.

I'm looking forward to getting the Polaroids of you and Doc.

Bob Hope doesn't get this far north and I was crushed but what can one do? War is hell. CHUCKLE.

Toombie, I want you to know that I really appreciate you and your letters and all those wonderful things that you do for lil ole Donny-poo. (Even though I feel that Patti is suffering somewhat.)

Seriously, you're great and I'm mighty proud to be…. Son of Toombie

Ta-tum-ta-tum-ta-tee!

§§§§§§§§§

I don't quite know what to say about these last few letters, written the last two weeks of December, 1967, the last Christmas he ever had.

I smile at "Give Patti some Amoco unleaded for me." Before Donn left, he had lectured us on why his car needed Amoco unleaded gas, which was by far the most expensive gas on the market at the time. The rest of the cars could burn leaded gas, but Patti had to have unleaded, <u>Amoco</u> unleaded.

As you have probably deduced, John G. was a neighbor of ours in Roanoke who worked in photography. He and his wife MM deserve a book of their own. Donn almost always references John when he talks about cameras or film or photography.

That 35 mm Canon was a great camera. To have bought it for $99., which made Donn gulp, makes me laugh out loud.

I inherited that camera, and I inherited Patti Porsche, too. Had I read these letters in the years immediately following Donn's death, I would have done better by both.

That camera was stolen from my house in Waco, Texas, sometime in the 1980s. I've never had one as good since.

Patti Porsche and I spent many years together, but we, too, separated in Waco, Texas. I could not afford to keep her in "primo shape," as Donn might say, and I could not afford to buy insurance for her in the event that she might be stolen. My husband and I, both in graduate school and living on rice and beans most of the time, struggled over the decision to sell the Porsche. We sold her to a doctor who was getting her all fixed up to give to his son upon his graduation from Texas A&M. Donn would have loved the fact that the doctor was willing to spend a lot of money to get Patti in beautiful shape again.

Do I even need to add here that I've never had another Porsche?

Letter 29

Envelope lost.
New Year's Eve

Hello Toombie,

Happy New Year and all that jazz. Received your letter of 23 Dec today. Sounds like you were prepared for Santy. Be sure and tell me all about Dockie's talk at church—I'm really anxious to hear about it.

Be sure and put SVC Btry on my address from now on. Thank you. Would you please send me a few special items when you get the chance? I'd like some black and white film that has a very fast speed (35 mm). Also some Murine eye drops, some peanuts that are still in the shell, a report on Patti and anything else you might find.... Good, sexy novels.

I'm really enjoying my new camera and although color slides would be nicer, B&W prints will be cheaper and I like to experiment.

I received a long letter from Boots in Germany, she's really a great girl and I enjoy hearing from her. Please put my latest letter from Howe and pay voucher away for me.

Do you think Doc needs a portable radio? That's about the only thing they sell here that I think she might like. If so, or if you'd like one, then do let me know. I guess R&R is going to be my only chance to buy presents for y'all.

Well, I'm at a loss for things to say.

Do take care and write soon.
Much love,

Donn

Letter 30

Postmarked Jan 6, 1968.
5 Jan

Hello Toombie,

It's Fri nite here and I'm sitting on my bunk listening to the radio. How goes it with my favorite Mom? Before I forget it, on that list of stuff I want (that I sent you) delete Murine and add Seald Orange Juice like you've sent before.

Since Xmas I haven't received much mail, guess everybody is recuperating from the festivities. Heard from Scott, Gib and Sukie (separate cards) the other day. Sounds like all is well with the Stones.

Next time you write Joan ask her to call the Atlanta Constitution (newspaper) and give them my new address. I just wrote her the other day and forgot to mention it. Thanks.

What have you been doing lately? Dockie will be home for semester break soon, won't she? Hope she does OK on her exams.

I didn't get my R&R for Bangkok so I'll be going to

Taipei (Formosa) for 5 days starting 2 Feb. I'm really excited about going – they say Taipei really swings. Did you see the Time article on R&R centers? GREAT! It was the Time with Bob Hope on the cover.

I'm starting to withdraw money from my bank account in anticipation of one big BLOW OUT.

Sounds like Lurleen Wallace has a bad time ahead of her.

I just now received your letter of 26 Dec with the three pictures. Doc REALLY LOOKS GOOD, and Toombs, you look thinner! The tree looks loverly and I feel homesick. Your stationery is hilarious.

Never did answer Myrna – my first failure to respond but it was just one of those things. You may verbally chastise me.

Sounds like Xmas was a busy and fun-filled day for y'all. Neatsy.

I'm still enjoying my camera, ask John G. to get me some fast B&W film and some fast color slide film (Ansco D-500). Plan to take many pix on my R&R as I think it's the only one I'll get. If you can get the film here before 31 Jan I'd be appreciative.

Still hear from Kathy – must be lonesome – says her life is dull. Problems.

I'm keeping quite busy here and rather enjoy my new job.

Now LISTEN Toombie, I insist on some answer about Patti. Oil changed correctly? Valve clearance checked? Battery OK? Tire pressure? Is she clean? Pretty? Lonesome? A clean bill of health from Gino or Runt or somebody will help put my mind at ease. How's the clutch?

Well, honey-Marion-B, take care of your bod and WRITE soon.

Luv,
SOT

P.S. Comment on acceptance into law school?

Letter 31

Postmarked Jan 18, 1968.

Below the flap, in Donn's handwriting:
"Received film and Playboy – many, many thanx."

16 Jan

Hello Toombie,

Last nite I received 2 letters from you, one from Joan and H&V, and 2 from Kathy. It was good to get mail after a 3 day absence.

As soon as I can I will send you a radio. I wish you'd let me know about things like that. What else could you use besides a watch? I may wait 'till R&R to purchase anything unless the PX here gets some decent goodies in. The other day I bought an electric toothbrush but I turned it in for a refund when I found out the power wasn't sufficient here to charge it. C'est la guerre.

The action over here has intensified with many convoys and outposts being shot up. This will probably last until TET (Buddhist New Year) which is about 31 Jan.

Doc's speech-talk sounded great. Good ole N-N-N. Hope she did OK on her exams. Speaking of school I'm organizing an educational program here (feel stale, intellectually) will probably teach 4 nites a week – freshman Eng and History. I think I'll be able to get 2 other officers to teach high school math and English and College Algebra. This is all via the U.S.Armed Forces educational program. Right now I'm signing up prospective students – my Battery Commander (Cpt Kruze) is one. Ho-ho. At any rate I hope it works out as it will be good for all concerned.

During the day (730 AM to 6-ish PM) I stay quite busy and dirty. The dust here is TERRIBLE, CHOKE! But, I rather enjoy my job – considering – and the time is going rather quickly.

Has the weather warmed up at all? Radio here said it was -26 degrees in Albany, NY. BR-R-R.

Did Dean Sutton ever call you from Rke College? I referred him to you for information as I needed a recommendation for school.

If you receive a roll of undeveloped 35 mm B&W film—please have it developed as I haven't been able to locate a place to send B&W film as yet. Bye the Bye, how are the Gilberts?

Sounds like Stu isn't long for this world – poor Bobbie. All these heart transplants are really something. Wonder what will be next.

Viv hinted in her letter that their next package will contain a bottle of Scotch --- yum-yum. Very hard to get Scotch up here.

My finances are kind of tight – most of my money goes to that car each month. At least when I get out of the Army it will be paid for – and I luv it. How is she today, anyhow?

Enclosed are a few more pictures – hope you find them interesting.

<u>DO</u> take care.
Love SOT

Letter 32

Postmarked Jan 25, 1968.
25 Jan

Hello Dockie and Toombie,

How are my goils today? Hope this gets there before Doc had to return to Duke.

I am now sitting at my desk playing "Battery Commander" and enjoying it veddy much. Since assuming command on the 18th I haven't gotten into too much trouble although I think the colonel will be happy to know I'm not making the Army my career.

Received your brownie "love" package and I 'tank you veddy much.' In fact I am now contentedly munching on Toombie's brownies and Jean P's goodies that I received in yesterday's mail. In fact, let me know if Jean mentions the thank you note I wrote her. I had great fun in writing it.

Here's another Happy Howzer letter—enjoy, enjoy!

I received my first slides that I took with my new camera. Will send them on, eventually. They came out very well. Proud of myself!

As I said before I received the film and Playboy – mucho gracias.

How's the weather now? Still snowed in? How's Patti? If you can't get her out to drive her, then do NOT just run the engine while it sits in the garage as the oil does not properly circulate and the engine isn't pulling anything. When will she go in to see Gino? Do you have a list of things I want checked?

Is Susan Baum in Rke now? Glad that y'all could have her down.

Yes, your mail usually comes in sequence, although that package of the film and Playboy came thru very fast.

Can understand, I guess, about your lack of enthusiasm for law school but it sounds better than just taking 'a job' when I leave here. Still haven't heard from Ga. Law school yet.

I did get a funny letter from Charles S.—he's a good friend.

Say Toombs, I want you to start thinking about what you intend to do with the house and furnishings etc. I'm going to have a slight problem as to what I'll do with all my furniture etc when I get out next Sept. If I go to Tucson or Athens or whatever I won't be able to set up an apt. for myself (too expensive) so I'll have to dispose of some of my accumulations. If it's all right with you I might have the stuff shipped to you in Aug or so and you could keep some things and sell others. For instance you might consider selling your sofa and a chair and taking mine instead. Anyway I want you to be thinking about the situation. Any way I look at it, I see a big mess on my hands. Too, I'll have to probably ship some of my things from Rke to wherever I do decide to go to school. Sigh!

Any chance you'll start work at GE soon? You must be kind of rocky, financially speaking, yes?

Too bad about Tom E's loss. You'd think an expensive school like that would have better facilities.

Wonder how Ruth and Ern are getting along. He wrote me a very business like letter stating he'd recommended me for McGeorge College of Law. Thought it a rather stiff note from ole Ern. Oh, well.

Will try to send you the book – it's now making the rounds around the battalion.

Take care kids,
D----------poo

P.S. Will look for jewelry for y'all.

P.P.S. Had a nice letter from Pris.

Letter 33

Postmarked Jan 31, 1968.
30 Jan

Hello Mom,

Just a note to let you know I'm OK. How are things with you? How's Dockie?

Received letters from H&V, Joan and Doc this week as well as packages from Mrs. Bowers, Kathy and you. Yesterday I sent a box to you. I hope it makes it OK. I sent you my first set of slides, the Exhibitionist, a radio and a telephone. The phone is something I was able to pick up and I can use it in the years to come so.... No portable radios are available up here so the one I sent you a friend of mine (Jack Sweeney) picked up in DaNang. I'll send another one soon (different type) and you and Doc can choose between them, OK? Let me know when it gets there and how the radio works.

Do not buy, or have Joan get, any Ga. license plates for my Porsche until I hear from Ga. Law School. If I'm rejected by them then it will be cheaper to buy Va tags.

Around the first of March I'll send you a check to cover my next life ins premium. Did you ever get the dividend payment changed?

The TET truce up here was cancelled (good) as the action is pretty fast and furious now. We've been cut off from the Rockpile for 6 days now – we're now forced to resupply them by air. Tell the Pritchards that one brigade of the 1st Cav is now at Quang Tri (10 miles south of here). (Bill P was with the 1st Cav – I think). We also have one battalion from the 101st Airborne – so you can see we're finally getting reinforcements up here. Every base up here has been hit in the last 7 days (except Dong Ha).

Take care.
Love,
SOT

My R&R starts in 5 days!

§§§§§§§§§

Sometime in the mid-1980s I was a visiting faculty member at Texas A&M University. In the course of that eighteen months I met a guy named Bud, who was dating a colleague of mine. Bud was a Vietnam vet, and I wanted to know what he thought about anything related to that.

Bud, with beer in hand and sounding very confident, explained to me that any guy who wanted to come home from Vietnam made it home. "It really wasn't that tough to survive. The guys who didn't make it weren't trying hard enough to make it."

My response to this comment was some semblance of catatonia.

Letter 34

Postmarked Feb 2, 1968.

Dong Ha
1 Feb
Late Thurs nite

Hello Toombie,

It's been a hectic 48 hrs and I'll give you a brief synopsis: Wed. I took an ammo convoy to the Rockpile (I was part of a bigger convoy which we call a Rough Rider convoy—Marine) and as you know the NVA/VC are active now. Well, we ran into an ambush and were mortared etc. Fortunately we only had 1 KIA (killed in action) and 1 WIA (wounded ....) We spent last nite at the Rock-- Today, coming back to Dong Ha we were hit again – very nasty business. After all this, Dong Ha got hit and it's a real bitch to get a flight out of here to DaNang now. I'll be trying though in about five and a half hours. Taipei here I come!

Received your Howard Johnson's note tonite. Stu was lucky to go so peacefully. How's Bobbie? What did H&V have to say? Did you call Goldstock?

Hope Bobbie appreciates all you've done for her.

How's my Dockie? Received a funny letter from her too – written after her German exam.

About med school ----- it was just an after thought (Ga's cheap and easier to get into) and so I applied. Don't think it will work because they wrote me and said they wanted to interview me. Hah! I suggested Saigon. We'll see. Not sure what I want. Was accepted into McGeorge College of Law in Sacramento – must let them know by 1 April. Ask Ernie what he thinks of McGeorge and U of Arizona, OK?

Plan to have a blast in Taipei – hope so anyway. Really anxious to get out of here for awhile. It's too hot here now. Fighting going on all over. What next, Korea?

We received our textbooks for teaching—will probably start about 15 Feb.

No electricity tonite and the candle is about gone so I'll bid adieu for now.

Take care and best of everything to you and my love to Dockie and Toombie.

Luv,
SOT

§§§§§§§§§

What kind of sign-off is that? "Take care and best of everything to you and my love to Dockie and Toombie." Sounds like a farewell.

The candle is about gone.

When my daughter read the first pages of this book, she said to me, "Wow, Mom, your letters must have been really funny." I suppose they were. Somewhere in me is a sense of humor, something I shared for a time with Donn.

In this letter he says, "How's my Doc?" What would he have thought of the depression that sank me like a stone after his death.

Occasionally humor pops back up in my personality, peeping up over the daily dose of Prozac that has kept me just this side of alive for decades.

Our mom has fared better. She has one amazing system, both biologically and emotionally. She survived the flu epidemic of 1918. Scientists want to look at her blood for super antibodies. She also survived the early death of her father and mother; the long, slow dying of her husband; the death of her son. Psychologists would no doubt like a peek at those survival systems.

Evelyn Sweet-Hurd

A few years ago I asked my husband why I couldn't be tougher; you know, "Have a tougher skin." He said, "Then you wouldn't be you."

The ironic thing is that most acquaintances think I do have a tough skin. Here's the news:

I don't.

Letter 35

Postmarked Feb 13, 1968.

Addressed to Mrs. A.L. Sweet. And in our mother's handwriting, the word "Instructions," underlined, on the envelope.

12 Feb

Happy Abe's BD!

Hello Mom, how are you? Just a note to let you know I'm back at Dong Ha and OK. Things have really been happening here—the lieutenant that replaced me as F.O. with the ARVNs (Steve Murden) was killed along with a few others last week. Mighty glad I'm no longer on A-1. Too bad about Steve. The war is really hot up here although Dong Ha is quiet. (Steve was hit on Hill #31.)

Received two packages from you – both were demolished. Please do not send crackers or candy in anything but tin cans or well-fortified boxes (strong plastic is OK). The chocolate covered nuts were scattered over everything and had melted. Guess you'd better stay away from stuff that melts.

Received 23 pix (B&W) you sent—hope the rest come soon. The guy Susan liked (dimples) was the one wounded in the fire that I took slides of – he's OK now.

Saw "Valley of the Dolls" in Taipei—enjoyed it too. Also "Point Blank" and "Wait until Dark."

Let me know how much money I have in my account after you cash this check, OK? This money is for life ins. premium and incidentals. Did the premium come yet? How much?

Mom, I sent two big items home – both are parts to my stereo system. They might come with US Duty (tax) due. If so, talk to them and find out how I can avoid paying it. Let me know what happens. They told me in Taipei that if I had enclosed my papers (orders for when I leave V.N.), then it would be duty free. If necessary they (Post Office) could hold the stuff until I get the orders. Do not pay the tax unless it looks like that would be the only way. The boxes should arrive about mid-March.

Haven't received the book yet – hope they didn't send it 3rd or 4th class. The mail is bad up here now anyway. How did Dockie end up for the fall semester?

Enclosed is a letter from Grace—kind of blah, yes?

By the way I loved the little pop-up doll you sent "Joy is…..sex!" What do you think of the fact that your son required 3.6 million units of penicillin after his R&R? Nasty! Ah, me! First a divorce and now VD. I've set the family back 200 years. Chuckle.

Received a remarkable letter from Chas Swartz—said that Ga. Law School is still undecided on me – if I don't hear by 24 March, then I'll say yes to McGeorge Law in Sacramento.

More in a few days – have much to do and must get busy.

Luv,
Donniepoo

P.S. Did ole Ern know anything about McGeorge Law?

§§§§§§§§§

There's a bit of relief. I had feared that the "Instructions" had to do with his wishes after death. It was good to see that he was thinking about his stereo system.

We still have the receiver that he bought. He purchased very good equipment. I don't know if Mom paid any tax or duty on it when it arrived.

Let me think a minute about his other instructions. Before he left for Vietnam, he told Mom and me that he would like to be buried in Arlington National Cemetery.

He is buried in the family plot in Schenectady, New York.

I have no idea how that happened. My uncle was a funeral director in Scotia, New York, and Donn's body was shipped there from Vietnam. I remember Uncle Howie (the "H" of H&V) telling us that he looked great and that we needed to see him before he was buried. Uncle Howie knew a thing or two about accepting reality and the possibility of closure.

We had a private, family-only viewing the evening before the burial. I remember thinking that it was indeed Donn, my Donn, lying there. He had a large bandage or something covering his neck, making his uniform bulge out a bit around the neck. He had on white gloves. Is that standard for military funerals? White gloves?

I kept thinking Donn would pop up out of the casket and crack a joke. "Aha!" he would say. "Gotcha!" But he didn't. He just lay there, still as a slab.

I spent a good bit of time that evening holding on to my brother-in-law, Tony. He seemed able to support me a little.

I don't recall anything else.

Letter 36

Postmarked Feb 16, 1968.
17 Feb

Hello Toombie,

How's my favorite Momma-san? We have very poor mail service up here since the war became so hot; therefore the latest letter I have from you is dated 4 Feb.

Received another letter from Charlie Swartz—said I've been accepted into Ga. Law. Guess I'll be a Georgia Peacher after all. I think that's where I'll go – haven't heard from Ga Med School yet, but I'm most undecided as to whether I should study law or medicine. After all this thought, I'll probably be rejected by med school anyway. Just as well – no doubt.

I sent Joan, Ginny, and Viv little gifts (brooches) from Taiwan. Hope they get there OK. [Sent Ginny and Viv similar pins....no favoritism that way].

Received a package from H&V. They sent me some food tidbit called "Poppycock" which was great. Hope they send more some day.

Have you received any of my packages yet? How's Patti? Has she been to see Gino yet? Write Joan and ask her for the forms or whatever to get new license tags for Patti.

Doc sent me a funny Valentine's Day card – sounds like she's doing fine.

Are you working much? Still GE? How's Bobbie? Where will Tim F. be stationed? How about filling me in about what you plan to do with the house etc (if anything). Guess I'll have to have my stuff shipped to Rke and then sent to Ga. again since I won't want it all.

Ginny wrote that she and Don may go to Hawaii next month to celebrate their 25th.

Take care Marion B. and please write.
Luv,
D. Lafayette

Letter 37

Postmarked Feb 28, 1968.

27 Feb

Hello Toombie,

Boy is this place screwed up! We've been mortared (sp), rocketed, and pounded with arty. The place is in a bind for supplies. We get mail about once every 4 days. I got your Feb 14th letter about 4 days ago; today I got your letter of Feb 10th! Had a letter from Joan. Really a shame about Jarret. Poor John and MM, no doubt they took it very hard.

How's the weather there now? I'm glad you got both your packages – sure hope my 2 boxes get there OK. Remember not to pay duty on them. (I hope).

You might as well keep the negatives from my B&W prints; I don't need them. Today I sent my movie film in – you ought to get it in about 3 weeks. When you show my movies you'll have to stop it occasionally because I take very quick, short shots so that I can conserve film. This roll ought to be something – has shots of Taipei, Gio Linh and the last few feet are of my newly painted Jeep (Says "Donnypoo") and of part of our ammo dump that was hit by enemy artillery (yesterday).

What's this about Dockie's roommate going to a headshrinker? N-N-N driving her nuts? [snicker.]

Does your radio pick up FM, OK? My history class may go down the drain – too much enemy action for now.

Yiddishly yours,
Irving Sweetstein

§§§§§§§§§

Another nickname: N-N-N. When I was little, I could not pronounce "Evelyn." And I have been "N-N-N" ever since, at least occasionally.

I had forgotten that little Jarrett drowned the year that Donn was in Vietnam. Two little boys from our neighborhood fell through the ice of a pond near our home. There's that haunting Vonnegut voice again.

How curious that Donn's history class was made impossible by enemy action.

Vietnam is history now. How many wars have we had since then? Bob Dylan is still singing, but we continue to have wars. Joseph Campbell said that we will always have wars, as that is part of who we are. Until I read that, I had been reading and researching for a solution to war. (What do English majors do? We search in books and re-search in books. We think we can find everything in written words, if we just keep searching.) But when I read Joseph Campbell's position that war is part of the human condition, I stopped looking for the magic that would eliminate war from life.

Part of our family mythos is that when Donn was born my dad said something to this effect: "It's 1942. He will have to fight in a war someday." Born during war, will fight in a war.

Will die in a war.

Letter 38

Postmarked March 2, 1968.
1 Mar

Hello Mummy,

Still alive and kicking; how are you? Received your letter of Jan 30th today! Boy, what a screw up. Also got a letter from Scott dated 30 Jan. His letter was a riot – he sent me $25 cash and told to "get a piece in Taipei" for him. What a character.

Received letters from Kathy, N-N-N, Dean Sutton of Rke College, Howard and Pris. We got mail for the 1st time in 6 days. Also got a smashed package from Ginny. Would you put my pay vouchers and Howard's letter away for me? Thanx.

I also got your picture postcard from Duke. Glad Doc liked her radio and pendant. How's your watch doing?

The war continues hot and heavy—we had one arty shell land close to my office – took pix of it. Nobody hurt as we were all underground.
I bought a Sony tape recorder from one of the guys so I can listen to some good music—will probably re-sell it before I leave in Aug.

I got an anonymous Valentine card signed "<u>ma</u> amour" from Rke. Think it was Jean P. If so, tell her the card was delayed 'cause she put the wrong APO #.

How's Patti? Still waiting for my status report. Do you know all that I want checked? Ask them how many miles I have left on the tires.

Well, that's about it for now. Just wanted to let you know I'm OK.

Toodle,
Son of Toombie

P.S. Sent a box of Army equipment to Pris' oldest boy Jim—6 yrs. She said he was at that stage.

§§§§§§§§§

Still alive and kicking on March 1 of 1968.

The P.S. of this letter brings thoughts, reflections. So the OLDEST child of the destroyed marriage of the other man was six years old. And he and Pris had five children. It would be interesting to hear from her, to learn perhaps that she found a wonderful man to share her life with, to help her parent her children.

The idea of Donn sending Army equipment to six-year-old Jim makes me smile. Donn was quite the soldier when he was a little boy. We lived in

Schenectady, NY, and in the backyard of our house was a trench Donn had dug for his Army activities. I was under no conditions ever to enter that trench.

In my eyes, that trench was huge and alluring in its danger. And of course it was forbidden for little sisters to go near.

Many years later, driving by our old house in Schenectady, I was astonished at the tiny backyard. How was there even room in that plot for the enormous trench, the scene of great battles?

When my son was young, he was not allowed to play with soldier toys, toy guns, GI Joe, toy tanks, or anything remotely resembling war. When other kids thought it was cool to wear camouflage, my kids were forbidden.

As Jeff grew older, he began to question how other kids could have toy guns and he could not. Even the sticks he picked up to wield as weapons were quickly removed by his quirky mom. I finally had to tell Jeff that much of the problem with toys of weaponry and war were my problem. That my brother had died in war, as a soldier, and I didn't see how any kind of war play was good in any respect. Jeff understood and stopped asking for that kind of toy.

When Jeff was in high school, he was participating in a superhero dress-up day at his school. He and one of his very best friends were going as characters from *The Matrix*. Jeff was the Keanu Reeves guy, and he needed some stuff that he thought he could find in the Army-Navy store in town. He asked me if I thought I could go there. I was feeling brave, so I said, "Sure!" After all, it was a store, for goodness' sake. And it was the year 2000.

We went in the store and I was perusing the goods when I came upon the racks of used Army boots.

I had had a pair of boots like that in my house for a while. Sent home with his effects, Donn's Army boots were so small that they looked like toy boots for the bigger boys.

Letter 39

Postmark unclear.

10 Mar

Hello Toombie,

How are things in Runamuck, VA? Still cold and wet? How's your health?

Ronnie S. is going to arty OCS, eh? Ugh. Tell Martha that if he wants to write me I'll give him some tips on how to get out. Naw, I wouldn't do that.

The other day I got your 2 packages. I appreciate the thoughtfulness of my favorite Toombie; however, the book The Lawyers I quickly sent back to you as I bought the same book in Taiwan and read it. I also have read Topaz by Uris. How about trying with another book? Can you exchange that one? How about The Confessions of Nat Turner? The cesspool tidbits and Playboy arrived OK. Many thanx.

By the way how much do I have in my bank accn't? Guess I'll send a check for my 2 speakers as the price goes up after 1 April. Money, money, where does it go so fast?

How are John and MM doing now? Tell MM I think I have a crush on her. *Snicker.*

Is Dockie going to Nassau? Wow-ee. How about JLB III?

The enclosed clipping is one that Ginny sent me – she requested I forward it to you. I barely recognized Tommy.

I read the <u>Adventurers</u> last yr. Very good – Harold Robbins really knows the story.

Hope Doc wasn't too disillusioned by my brush with VD (think I told her). Anyway that was taken care of within 36 hrs. No problem.

The war up here isn't going too well – we need to unleash all our power and defeat the Gooks PDQ. One of my ammo "humpers" was hit by some artillery about 2 weeks ago or so and lost his right arm. Other than that we roll merrily along.

Received a nice note from H&V and Sukie Stone. Howie also sent me a pint of scotch packed in a loaf of bread. So funny.

Take care and write soon,
Donniepoo

§§§§§§§§§

Now that I think about it, I don't know what Donn majored in in college. He earned his bachelor's degree from Roanoke College, and he went to University of Virginia for a year or two to add some post-graduate work in science. At that time he was still focused on getting into medical school.

He always wanted to make money someday. When medical school didn't look like it would pan out, he shifted to law.

I had forgotten that March of 1968 was when I was heading to Nassau with my friend Jane for Spring Break. Two college sophomores, from Wake Forest and Duke, making the big trip to the Bahamas. I did not think about the war that week.

Donn hopes that I wasn't too disillusioned by his brush with VD. I was. I was absolutely disgusted, horrified, and disillusioned.

I was nineteen years old.

Letter 40

Postmarked March 15, 1968.
13 Mar

Hi there Toombie,

Received your letter of 26 Feb tonite as well as letters from H&V, Kathy, and a card from Ginny. Also packages from Jean P. and Sukie S.

Glad to hear Patti is in such fine shape. Hope you saved the bill so I can keep a record of what I'm spending on her and what parts she's getting. Hope she's OK—how about her tires?

I did receive your can of Danish butter cookies—very tasty as well as the cesspool tidbits.

Tomorrow I take a convoy to the Rockpile—don't expect too much trouble.

Will send the latest H. Goldstock letter soon – he's so funny and a real friend.

Fear that I'll need to see a dentist PDQ once I'm able to see one again.

The rumor is that I'm being "infused" soon. That means that I'll be sent to another unit so that this unit will not lose so many officers at one time. I know that probably doesn't make sense to you – but anyway it looks like I may leave here and go to the Americal Division – time will tell.

Today I bought two speakers for my stereo set up which should get there in about a month or two. Keep me informed.

Well, that's about all for now. Give my luv to one and all.

Toodel, woops, Toodle,
Donniepoo
Son of Toombie

P.S. The Americal Division is the biggest in Vietnam and is spread out throughout central V.N.

§§§§§§§§§

I suppose every family has funny little family jokes. My sister Joan had named a favorite dessert "cesspool tidbits" in hopes that that would deter people from eating them. They are divine little treats of chocolate chips and coconut and crushed graham crackers and condensed milk.

I don't understand this "infused" business. He would be sent to another unit so that his unit would not lose so many officers at one time? Does that mean that his unit was losing officers – as in KIA – more than other units? Was there a quota or percentage that Army officials kept track of?

I suppose I could ask an Army person about this. One guy I met at my high school reunion a few weeks ago. I had not known him well at all in high school, and I had not even known that he had been to Vietnam. I was telling him about Donn's letters and this book, and I was wishing we had more time to talk. When I told him Donn had been killed in late July of 1968, and that his orders to come home were being processed for August, he told me that guys like Donn were called "Short timers."

Another Army person I know is a real estate person here in Conyers, GA. He is a graduate of West Point and he served in Vietnam. He is currently in Iraq. I had not even realized he had gone to Iraq until I sent out a mass e-mail about summer swim teams, and he replied with, "Hello from Baghdad!"

He felt the call to go back to duty.

Amazing stuff. I don't understand it.

I wonder if his wife and teenaged children do. His daughter is at West Point now, so probably she does. Would he want her there in Iraq? Does that potential sacrifice make sense to him?

Letter 41

Postmarked March 20, 1968.

19 Mar

Hi Toombie,

Help! I need your assistance PDQ. Here's my problem: I ordered 2 speakers for my stereo and paid by check which left me with about $8. in my account. So today I received a letter (which you forwarded) from Ga. Law which states that they want a $50. deposit by 1 April '68. So-o-o, I'm sending said check and hope that you will deposit $50.00 in my account at once! Hate to start my law school career with a bad check. Many thanx.

Sent your 2nd book back today. So funny! You bought the same two books I did. At least you sure know my tastes. I'll not buy any more. By the way don't send any more packages until I send you my new address. I'll be moving soon, I'm not sure exactly where or when but think it will be with the 9th Inf Div which operates in the Delta and near Saigon. As soon as I know I'll let you know.

Doc hasn't written lately so haven't heard anything about Eugene. Interesting to note I received my first letter from JLB III today. Ho ho.

You never did answer the question about changing my ins. policy concerning dividends. What's happening to the dividends now?

Raining like hell here now.

Patti's bill wasn't too bad. Hope she's running as well next Sept. I expect to get in the US about 10 Sept.

Had a nice letter from David S. Said he enjoyed Gene McCarthy. Typical. Bobby K sure has thrown a monkey-wrench into things, yes? Ho-ho. I like a Nixon-Javits ticket. You?

Asked Joan to get my plates yet?

Think Ga. Med School will accept me (they're still writing me), but I've about convinced myself that I'd be happier in law and eventually politics (maybe). Probably make more money in medicine but takes too long and there's lots of money in law too.

More letters soon,
Luv,
SOT

P.S. Don't forget the $50.00 deposit please.

§§§§§§§§§

There it is. He expected to return to the US about September 10th.

And Bobby Kennedy was throwing a monkey wrench into politics.

After Donn died, I unraveled pretty much. I recall singing two songs at the top of my lungs whenever I could sing alone-- in the shower, walking in the rain. The first was "He Ain't Heavy, He's My Brother," and the second was "Abraham, Martin, and John."

Did you see a skinny girl singing loudly and not well as she walked through the rain in the streets of Richmond, Virginia, in the 1970s or 80s? Was she bellowing something about brothers and Abraham and Martin and Donn?

Probably me.

Letter 42

No postmark.

23 Mar

Hi Toombs,

Well, it's been one helluva day. Took a convoy to the Rockpile and we were mortared on the way out (mild) and took rockets at the R—pile. All very exciting-- no one was hit.

My B.C. (Cpt Kruse) complained to the colonel about me being transferred so he changed it and now I stay here. Blah! Just as soon have moved and met new people and seen new places. Oh well.

Had a letter from Doc yesterday. She mentioned Eugene. Kind of funny.

My bank account is all screwed up—I figure I have -$62, that's minus sixty-two dollars. Must have beaucoup checks outstanding.

Here's Howe's latest. Quite a guy.
My best to all and write soon.

Evelyn Sweet-Hurd

Luv,
S.O.T.

P.S. Had a letter from Pris—she's fine.

P.P.S. It's really hot here now!

P.P.P.S. Try to number my movies so I have them in sequence.

Letter 43

Postmarked March 29, 1968.
27 Mar

Hi Toombie,

Received your letter of the 15th tonite. 12 days! So glad the movies came out OK. The girls <u>were</u> cute—I like slant eyes anyway, as you know. The tracked vehicle I was driving is used by us to carry ammo in. It's like a two and a half ton truck on tracks.

Did my other box of stereo equipment come yet? Sure hope so. So glad you didn't have to pay duty on it.

Your comments about Judy C. were a riot. I wonder where Eric is these days. Next time you're near Kingoff's Jewelers stop in and ask Mrs. H. about him. Thanx.

Your refresher course in nursing sounds like a good idea. Let me know how it goes.

Sure hope Patti stays in good condition—
Joan has written me quite regularly—sure is nice of her. Mail takes on added importance when things get a little hot around here.

More and more troops are moving up this way and especially to the area just south of the Rockpile, near CaLu.

John M. is the one who impregnated Mickey. He was in my class.

Did I tell you that Stetson Law accepted me? So I was accepted into all 4 schools—guess veterans have a sympathetic ear.

Had a letter from Ginny yesterday. She said Tom was still on the proverbial med-school fence. Sure hope he gets in; otherwise he may end up in this mess. She said Bill was going to Daytona over Spring Break "….hope he doesn't get put in jail." Good ole Ant Virginny.

I received a very concerned letter from Penny (Ben P's secretary) and the others in Ben's office asking about me. Anyway I wrote them (yesterday) and told Ben that I'd be going to law school next fall instead of returning to insurance. Wonder how he'll take that bit of information.

Well my lights are about to go out so I'll bid you adieu for now.

Toodle,
Me

P.S. Big operation starts 1 April.

Letter 44

Postmarked March 30, 1968.

29 Mar

Hi Toombs,

Am sending about 80 slides to you with brief explanations of each slide – hope you enjoy them. The girl I call Ginny was really nice and I spent most of my time with her.

This picture is my favorite so far – looks like the real-boy type, yes?
I forgot H&V's BD and anniversary—sorry. When you see Joan over Easter give her my best and ask her about inquiring about whether or not I'll be able to vote in the Nov election.
Big operations going on up here – the D-Day for the push to Khe Sahn is 1 April. Activity is heavy but Dong Ha is quiet.
Well, that's all that's new for now.
Toodle,
D--------poo
P.S. My other stereo box come from Taiwan yet?

Evelyn Sweet-Hurd

§§§§§§§§§

Amazing to me that he could write things like "the D-Day for the push to Khe Sanh is 1 April." I had no idea soldiers could write information like that in letters and have it go through the mail. I suppose a former version of myself, the one who used to research anything and everything, or the later one who had her students do the research for her, would investigate the way mail was handled in Vietnam in 1968. No censorship at all? No "loose lips sink ships"?

But the current version of myself is barely interested. My thoughts go to a TV personality getting in trouble for scratching out in the sand a US military position in Iraq on TV.

Donn was very interested in politics and wanted to vote in November of 1968. He was a Nixon fan. I can barely keep my breakfast down, writing that. Of course I have the advantage – or disadvantage – of knowing what Nixon did in his years in office. Would Donn think it amusing that dear ol' Duke refused to put Nixon's portrait up in the Law School? Wouldn't he laugh at the shenanigans of Watergate?

We have mid-term elections here tomorrow. I will go vote. In two years I will vote in another presidential election. Will it be John Edwards vs. John McCain? Speculation about candidates is already fascinating to CNN junkies.

158

Donn would have loved it. I wonder, had he lived through his war, how he would feel about the war in Iraq.

No doubt he would not be surprised that we are in another war. But I bet he could never have imagined the events of 9-11-2001.

I stop. The connection between the events of 9-11 and the war in Iraq is virtually none, but I have linked them in the previous two sentences. To follow the dots, we would have to see that only George W. Bush and Dick Cheney and a few of their circle thought the US should attack Iraq as a consequence of 9-11.

I had so hoped to write this book without mentioning Bush and Cheney.

With war, we must also concern ourselves more than usual with politics. The mid-term elections are over, and the American public has told "W" that his war on Iraq stinks.

The biggest news, however, may be the resignation of Donald Rumsfeld. Military generals, among many others, have called for Rumsfeld to get out for a long time. Surprisingly, Bush has now done that. And almost the first thing I heard on CNN was a comparison between Rumsfeld and McNamara.

Evelyn Sweet-Hurd

Robert McNamara. Secretary of Defense when Vietnam was our war. Many years later, decades later, he actually admitted he had been wrong about Vietnam. His own family had turned against him, if I am recalling correctly. Somehow, McNamara found he could not live with himself and he finally told the public that he regretted sending American men and women to die in a war he knew was already lost. He apologized.

When McNamara made his feelings known, I wanted to locate him personally. I wanted to either strangle him or just stand in front of him and cry until he drowned.

Letter 45

No envelope.

2 Apr, scratched out, then "Tues nite" written in.
Hello Momma-Tom,

Here are a few things I'd like you to save. Today I received 2 letters from you dated the 19th and 24th of March.

Sounds like your weather is a little mixed up—how is it now? The books took so long to get here because the stores sent them 4th class which means they go by boat across the Pacific. My bank account still is screwed up—I figure I have about $150. Oh well!

Good to hear that you're taking such good care of Patti for me.

The box arrived here tonite also—the nuts and OJ came thru OK. The glass peanut butter (crunchy, too!) was a mess. I almost cried. Someday how about scooping out a jar and transferring the stuff to a plastic or tin? C'est la guerre.

Have not received the magazine and placard.

Glad you and Louise are having so much fun—guess she's as nutty as my favorite Toombie.

Gene sounds like a nice guy-- how's the romance coming along?

Surprised to see that Steve is marrying Sally. Ho-hum.

Tell John I'm looking forward to the party—I assume my date will be MM. Everyone is sans clothes and is doused in Wesson Oil and then it's just a big party-orgy. Fun?

Sure hope RFK isn't nominated. Think Dirty Dick is the best. What's the scuttlebutt there? My subscription to Time ran out and mail is so lousy here anyway.

Dong Ha is still shelled occasionally—but not near us. Things are relatively quiet. We're moving one helluva lot of men and supplies in this part of I Corps now.

Next package, could you send me some white athletic (cotton) socks?

Joan sent me a tape which I received yesterday—very good. Must write her soon.

Well, that's it for now—Take care.
Luv
SOMT
Son of Mamma Tom

§§§§§§§§§

RFK.

I cannot wait to see a new movie that is coming out this month: <u>Bobby.</u>

I don't recall how I felt about RFK in April of 1968. I vividly recall his assassination.

The Kennedy stories are beyond imagination. When John F. Kennedy, Jr., died in a plane crash a few years ago, it was surreal. What must his sister feel?

I am searching for the word that describes my feelings as I read Donn's letter about crunchy peanut butter. He almost cried. I can see him looking at a mess of broken glass and crunchy peanut butter and realizing it is beyond salvage. I can almost hear his sighing. And it makes me sad that he wanted it so badly.

Letter 46

Postmarked April 14, 1968.

Passover

Happy Passover/Easter Toombie,

How was your trip to Atlanta? How's Joan looking these days?

Forget about sending me any peanut butter; 2 days ago I received a lg jar of Skippy from Pris—pretty nice of her.

I enjoyed your card. Haven't heard from Doc recently—tell her to write once more before exams, OK?

Had an amusing letter from Tom —said he thinks he missed med school. He's worried about the draft, natch. Can't blame him. I'm glad I'll have that behind me when I start law school. I'm to register for school on 22 Sept. Things will be rushed but that's how it goes. My biggest problem will be getting my belongings shipped from Columbus to Rke and then getting what I want back to Athens. I'm trying to get Charlie Swartz to line me up an apt and some roommates as I'd hate to live in a dorm—not too hopeful, though.

Just read <u>To Sir, With Love</u>, excellent.

The war is as usual over here—that is it's still hot and heavy up here although Dong Ha remains quiet.

I finally received your plaque—it now graces my wall—lovely.

The weather has turned from 90 plus degrees to mid 60s and wet. Nothing is dry now and we can only hope that the sun will shine again soon.

Five months from today I should be a civilian again—hooray!

For future reference, if anyone would like to know what I'd like for a birthday present or a "get-out-of-the-f---king Army gift" just advise them that I need clothes. All types.

How's Patti these days? How is the nursing profession progressing? What are your plans for the summer and next fall?

Well, do write and take care.
Son of Toombie

§§§§§§§§§§

Happy Passover and Easter! Nice combination of Old and New Testament greetings.

When we were growing up in Schenectady, we were fairly lonely Protestants in a sea of Catholics and Jews. We celebrated the Jewish holidays. I remember sitting at the table with my best friend Susie and her family as they tried to explain to me various things about unleavened bread and gefilte fish, and expecting a guest at the table. Donn, of course, had the Goldstocks.

In Roanoke, I wondered where all the Jews were. I think I knew one, and he didn't even go to my high school.

Our cousin Tom did indeed get into medical school. He has had an impressive career in oncology. Tom inherited the Berning balding gene, as did Donn. Tom has lived long enough to see that genetic trait come to fruition, if balding can be said to do that. At 26, Donn had a hairline that suggested that balding would be coming along later. If there had been a later.

Imagine going from Vietnam to dorm-life. How bizarre would that be.

A while ago I had a student at the Savannah College of Art and Design who was a Gulf War veteran. Gulf One, I guess we are calling that war now. The student was in his mid-twenties, and he was a remarkable writer and artist. But he could never sleep, and I worried about him. I would ask him outside of class to talk to me a bit, but he would not. He only said once, in an essay, that he had been standing next to his best friend when that best friend was blown into a million pieces in the war. Much worse than glass and peanut butter. Nothing left to salvage.

Just how is someone supposed to live with that?

That same student was in a class with me when we studied Catch-22. He understood that book better than anyone.

Donn would have absolutely loved that book. The wicked humor, the crazy Army logic. Yossarian's rocky sanity after the bombardier bled out.

Of course I barely can state the irony here of this sentence that Donn wrote: "My biggest problem will be getting my belongings shipped from Columbus to Roanoke and then getting what I want back to Athens."

No, Donn. That wasn't the biggest problem.

And the Army shipped all of your belongings to Roanoke. None of it had to go on to Athens, Georgia. It all sat in our garage in our split-level home on Walmann Road for a long time. It was mute. So were we.

Letter 47

No envelope.

Fri nite the 19th

Hi Toombie,

How's my favorite Mater? You really are top drawer, Toombs. I appreciate your frequent missives.

This past Mon, Tues, and Wed I was about 20 miles S.E. of Dong Ha at a place called Utah Beach. We went there to get some supplies that the bn needs. Anyway while there it was hot and sunny so we spent many hours on the beach. I went swimming and body surfing. It was great and I got sunburned—my nose is now peeling (pealing?)

Currently I'm running convoys between Dong Ha and C-1. Things are relatively quiet here. Khe Sanh has been cleared—the NVA cleaned out—guess they've pulled back to recover and let their supplies build up during the restricted bombing. As soon as LBJ finally gets his head extracted from his colon and realizes that Ho is still full of fight, then the better off we'll be.

Did you get my license plate? Find out anything about my voting status for Nov?

Received a long letter from Doc—it was good to hear from her.

Jean P. sent me some goodies among which was a can of grapefruit sections—fabulous. Love fruit, especially peaches, pears, and g—fruit sections. Anyway I sent her a thanx note.

Today I got a cordial letter from Ga. Med saying they could not accept me for this Sept because they could not interview me but wanted me to reactivate my application for Sept 69. Good luck! Wish they had accepted me so I could have turned them down since I'm convinced that law is more my cup of tea.

Have my speakers come yet? Also 2 boxes from Taiwan?

You should have asked Sen. Percy about his dove-like attitude on Vietnam. He doesn't impress me too favorably—seems a little too saintly.

Sure hope you're saving and collecting all my slides, pix and movies so that I'll have them all when I get back. How do you like these lovelies? These were killed in the TET offensive in DaNang.

Too bad Peg isn't in Patti's class, but that's the way it

goes. Sure hope Patti is doing well and is well taken care of.

Haven't received your Easter card yet. What about Passover? Had another funny letter from Goldstock.

The Army is worse than ever over here. Too much chicken shit and the overall policy of no-win (shades of Truman and Korea) leads to the sum total of low morale.

Well, I only have about four and one-third months left.

Take care.

Love,
D---------poo

§§§§§§§§§

Actually, my sweet brother, you had about three months left when you wrote that letter. None of us knew it at the time.

I wonder if God knew it. Does God know all things? We are obviously trapped in our linear time. Looking through a glass darkly and all that.

Someone said that we have a birth date and a date of death, with a dash in-between, and it's that dash in-between that is important.

But the mystery of death is fascinating, isn't it? It would be wonderful to be able to concentrate on the dash of the present, the moment of being alive here and now, but we cannot help but wonder at the transition through death. To what?

These are the questions for philosophers and theologians, but they are questions for the rest of us, too.

Meanwhile, back in the war, Donn was commenting on LBJ and the overall no-win policy of the war, comparing it to Truman and Korea.

Lt. Sweet was definitely a hawk. Maybe a hawk and a half.

Was it Barry Goldwater who wanted to bomb North Vietnam back to the Stone Age?

The letter we received from the President of the United States giving us his condolences regarding Donn's death was signed Lyndon B. Johnson.

Not too long ago I saw a documentary film that showed LBJ's agony over Vietnam. He wanted to be a president who did wonders for Civil Rights, and he instead had to deal with the crazy war in Vietnam. Hey, hey, LBJ, how many kids did you kill today?

It was a little gratifying to know that he agonized over Vietnam.

I did not know the soldiers knew that we had a "no-win" policy. How do you send soldiers to fight and die for that?

Letter 48

Postmarked April 25, 1968.
Wed nite 24 Apr

Hi Marion B,

Received your letter and card from Atlanta yesterday. The card was hilarious. Trust you are safely back in R---e Va now. How's Pat?

How did Cindy like Duke or don't you know? Sorry I missed Ant Virginny's BD but you don't give me enough warning. Hope you didn't send <u>The Arrangement</u> as I read that last yr. Send NEW books, if any. Hate to see you waste money like that.

What I really need is some Ocusol or something similar to wash the dust out of my eyes. Can't wear my lenses 'cause of that, thus the Ocusol.

Things are about the same here. We're hauling ammo like mad in preparation for the probable mess ahead once they quit "negotiations."

My car insurance expires in June. Let me know if they send any literature or bill etc as I want to renew it if the price is right.

Evelyn Sweet-Hurd

Well, must run.

Toodle,
Kid-Kid

Letter 49

Postmarked May 4, 1968.

May Day

Hi Toombie,

I talked to you this morning and it was great to hear the Fabulous Toombie Voice. I'm proud of you for tackling nursing again—Is it wearing you out? Take it slow and easy.

Funny to hear about Tombo and daughter—most of my

[Letter stops abruptly here.]

Hello again—

It's now 3 May and I'll try to scratch off a fast letter to you before I'm hustling ammo again. The last week has been really hectic—The NVA are just outside our perimeter and the war has become very hot and heavy up here. We've been working nite and day moving ammo. The jets and gunships are constantly bombing and machine gunning. C-1 position has been isolated from Dong Ha for about 6 days and that's only about 2 miles north of here. It's really uncanny how we can sit here and watch a war progress before our eyes. The Marines took some heavy casualties yesterday but Dong Ha Combat Base is relatively safe. I've never worked so long and hard without let up before-- Ah me.

H&V sent me another "loaded" loaf of bread—very nice of them. Also got a letter and package from Pris— she seems to be doing fine.

Enclosed is my small claim to fame—a letter of appreciation from Westmoreland that was passed down to us. Big deal---- ho ho. Actually not many officers get this and I was the only lt. as far as I know.

Please put the pay voucher away for me.

Do take care – must run now and I enjoyed talking to you and will try it again some time.

Toodle
Donniepoo

Letter 50

Postmarked May 13, 1968.

Happy Toombie (Mother's) Day!!

12 May

Hi Toombs,

Working like the devil still and no let up in sight. 1st Cav is up here in strength and taking heavy casualties. Sure hope this breaks soon as my men are exhausted. Went to C-1 yesterday without incident. Owe several people letters but don't have the time to write and when I do I'm too tired.

I received your box with socks etc.; many thanx—it came thru in good shape.

Glad to hear your school work is agreeable with you. Nurse Sweet, eh?

So glad that my speakers came—just hope I have a place to put them. I don't know where I'll live come Sept.

Had a letter from Dockie—she sure was teed off at J &T about the Easter incident in Rke. Ah me! How about she and Gene this summer? Keep me posted.

Please put this Playboy receipt in my box. Well, do take care and write often.

Luv,
Your favorite son—Son of Toombie

Letter 51

Postmarked May 18, 1968.

17 May

Hello Toombie and Doc (if you're there),

Started to write a letter to Doc but didn't know when she'd be leaving Duke so.....

Things are fine here in Douche Town, Vietnam. The "bad guys" in the black hats have gone away for the time being and things have quieted down. The weather is hot and dusty and generally miserable.

Your package of grapefruit sections (delicious), OJ (thanx) and the latest Playboy and dirty paperback came in good shape. Must send John a thank you note for his loverly book.

As it stands now I should be arriving in Oakland, Calif. about Sept. 4th or 5th. Sure hope it works out that way as I'm anxious to get back to civilization and get started in law school. Speaking of law, tomorrow I have a court martial and I'm the trial counsel or prosecutor. Ho ho. Ought to be rather funny.

The day before yesterday Cpt Kruse my BC sent me to the Battalion Commander for disciplinary action as I've been giving him a hard time on a number of things. Well, the new colonel and I hit it off just fine and he told me he wished he had a BC slot open as he'd like to give me a battery to command because I "obviously needed more responsibility." Anyway the colonel and I are on the same wave length (almost) and Kruse is in the doghouse. Too bad these Cpts can't learn to leave me alone. Chuckle.

Will try to have my furniture sent to Rke in August. As I said before, sell the large items like couch, chair, table, bed etc if you want or keep and sell yours. Do not sell the dishwasher or rug. Chas S. wrote and said he still hasn't found a place for me to live next fall. Fudge! By the way he just got married – rather sudden.

Well, must run—will con't this later.
Me

9:50 p.m.

Later—

Hi again. Just finished checking the guard and it's too hot to sleep. Enclosed is my letter to the editor—how about that? First letter of that type I've ever written.

Tomorrow is Uncle Ho's BD—hope we don't get shelled again.

Say, you sent me eye drops a la Murine. What I need is Ocusol to wash out my cute little eyes. Anyway forget it now as it's too dusty to bother with.

Still hoping to get a second R&R but it's doubtful right now.

Well, guess that's about it for now.

Toodle,
Donniepoo

P.S. Today's high was 103 degrees in the shade.

§§§§§§§§§

Oh, Donn. This letter is so full of your voice. "Douche Town, Vietnam." The enemy as the guys in black hats. Appreciation for a dirty paperback book. And later, an expletive: "Fudge!" Some expletive.

I wonder what could be amusing about a court martial. I bet it wasn't so funny for the soldier who was the defendant.

The paragraph about Cpt Kruse sending Donn for disciplinary action gives me great pause. As I recall, Donn is sent into the field as a forward observer as a punishment in late July. I guess I will have to wait to see if the letters of July talk about that. My memory tells me that he was killed while being heroic as a

183

Forward Observer, a duty he wasn't supposed to have at that time.

I started to say "at that stage of the game." Some game. If he was sent out as a disciplinary action, his punishment was death. I would have to wonder if his superior officer felt anything about that. I would have to wonder, too, if that officer would realize that Donn wasn't the only one who was "punished."

My brother and I have always had a penchant for offending authorities. I have more than once been referred to as "not a team player." In high school I got sent home for receiving too many demerits, most of which came for talking back to teachers. Yes, that was the very demerit system that Donn had inspired when he frolicked the halls of Cave Spring High School.

I have always considered myself a dandy team player. I just want to be the one who tells the rest of the team what to do.

Letter to Editor

U.S. Is Welcome Aid in Vietnam

APO San Francisco -- I am writing in response to the letter which appeared in The Atlanta Constitution of March 15.

Mr. C.C. Wiggin assails our being here in the Republic of Vietnam and seems to think that nearly all South Vietnamese are VC sympathizers. According to Mr. Wiggin the "non-Communists Vietnamese Nationalist" is a rare bird indeed. May I suggest that Mr. Wiggin visit Vietnam, especially the villages and towns located in northern South Vietnam? I do not claim to be an authority on the current pulse of the average Vietnamese sentiments, but I have lived and worked with some of them and I can only relay what they have said to me. To say that they are suffering immeasurably yet willing to continue the struggle to drive out and defeat the Communists is an understatement.

If the situation here were as Mr. Wiggin presents it, then our job would be much more difficult than it is. The fact is that the people of South Vietnam are, by in large, very happy that we are here and lend us tremendous assistance. They have told me that the United States, unlike France and China before her, is a welcome ally and not a necessary evil.

I think many of us here just south of the DMZ would welcome the opportunity to discuss the situation face to face with people such as Mr. Wiggin and Sen. Robert Kennedy. It would be a pleasure to let them see for themselves how wrong they are. Besides a few of us here are a little tired of Radio Hanoi quoting Sen. Kennedy to us.

D.L. Sweet
1st LT. ARTY.

Letter 52

Postmarked May 28, 1968.
Addressed to "The Sweet Girls."

27 May

Hello Toombie and Dockie,

It's another horrible day here in Dong Ha. The heat and dirt are unbearable. Everyday it's windy and in excess of 100 degrees. Everything is dirty and hot. Too, the NVA have started raising hell again and that adds to the general discomfort. No kidding, this heat is the worst I've ever experienced and there is NO relief. We have ice occasionally so every so often we have a cool drink. I'm losing weight (a little) and my lovely head of beautiful hair is disappearing....shades of Alva I suppose.

So glad to hear that your nursing course is coming along so well. When do you finish?

What are you doing Dockie? What about Gene?

I sent home a box of odds and ends, plus pix. Will send more as the time to leave approaches as I want to carry a small bag when I do depart. Just took some more movies to show y'all the wind and dust plus some jets in action—as I said the Gooks are back around Dong Ha.

Still could use more white cotton sox-- just like the others would be fine.

J&T's new home looks nice—will you be visiting them soon or vice-versa?

Within two weeks I will have to decide where to have my stored furniture, etc., sent. It will go either to you or to J & T. What do you think? I plan to sell most of the furniture (except rug and dishwasher) as I'm tired of lugging it place to place and I'll need $. Do you want anything? Do call Joan and discuss and let me know ASAP.

Is Ron S. in OCS yet? Will get in touch with him when he does so I can sell some uniforms.

How did you do this semester, Doc? What will you take next fall? How does Gene like law? In what fields is he interested?

Your letters are now taking about 11 -15 days to get here. Hope that changes soon.

The clipping is from the Atlanta Constitution—when I get home I'll tell you about it.

Are you keeping my movies in order of appearance? Want to put them on one big reel. Forgotten what I've taken pix of by now.

Feel sure the Talks in France are worthless. The thought of RFK in power is frightening to us. Millions of Viet kids would die if we quit or pull out. We ought to be here, but should fight offensively, not this way.

My stomach is so messed up—can't wait till I get out of here.

Really don't feel as if I can afford another R&R but I'll take one if I can—just to be out of this rat race and be cool and clean for a change.

Well, anyhow—what's new with y'all? Any travel plans for the summer?

I've met some very interesting guys over here—think wars are great for a very limited number of reasons.

Guess that about brings you up to date, be sure to take care of Patti for me and write soon.

Luv,
SOT
BOD (Brother of Dockie)

P.S. BD gift suggestion for me: wallet and clothes and floor mats for Patti. Hold all till Sept. Ta-ta.

Letter 53

Postmarked May 31, 1968.

30 May

Hello Toombie,

Just received your letter of 18 May—mail from Atlanta gets here about 6 days faster—Rke is slow I guess.

Wrote quick notes to Cindy E. and Howard G. today—enclosed is Howzer's latest. Luv that plaque. Please place in my file.

It rained here yest. And today—what a relief! Didn't last long but it hinders the dust.

Sounds as if you're staying plenty busy. Good for you. How's Dockie and Patti? Tell Audrey F. those "ditty bags" are much appreciated over here if they get to the guys in the field.

Hope Dockie's grades didn't suffer too much.

Wonder how rough it will be for me to get back in the swing of academic things. Still don't have a place to live—sigh. Where do you want my furniture sent? Do tell, PDQ.

Did Tom E. ever get into med school? Sent Cindy a button that said "Warning: Pornographic literature can make you pregnant," bet Ginny will love that!

When I get home in Sept do you plan a ticker tape parade down Walmann Rd? How about inviting some people over for a drink?

I have about 95 days left now and I'm really looking forward to getting out of here.

Decided to sell my tape recorder because it was getting too dirty and electricity is very erratic here – we more often than not don't have any.

Met this one guy here, Rollie Cook from W.Va (originally) who's Joan's age. Really a great guy—he helps make this place bearable as Cpt Kruse is such a hillbilly dufo—unfortunately Cook leaves here in 6 days. C'est la guerre.

Can't figure out why I'm so broke—sure will be a tight squeeze next year. GI Bill will help tremendously. Guess I'll cash in my life insurance or something. Hope to get a couple hundred out of the furniture and stuff. Imagine Patti needs tires and battery too. Anyway it will be interesting.

Well, guess that's about it for now—take care of your bod Toombs and write soon.

D-------------poo

§§§§§§§§§

Remember those books that had "Dear Reader" as the way the author would address the reader?

I feel compelled to use that device here.

Dear Reader,

That is the last of the letters from May. I do not want to pick up the June letters, because I know that the letters stop in July.

I have tried to prepare myself. I have e-mailed a few friends to expect a melt-down when I get to the July letters.

The other part of me is curious to know what he wrote in June and July. Obviously, in May he was already talking a great deal about when he would be home.

Ninety-five days! A ticker tape parade!

Hey, Donn. How about 55 days and a funeral?

It has been at least a week since I have written anything. It is now Thanksgiving Day, 2006, and I know that if I am to complete this book, I must include the letters of June and July.

Remember Donn's letter from Thanksgiving of 1967? Happy Turkey Day.

Here in 2006, the news lately has been absurd. President George W. Bush, noted for his dubious service in the National Guard during the Vietnam War, has gone to Vietnam for a visit with leaders there. Stand up comics are having a field day: "He asked his dad to get him out of it, but he couldn't"—that sort of thing. Ted Koppel, visiting Jon Stewart on <u>The Daily Show</u>, said Bush "went to Washington to stay out of Vietnam in the '60s, and now he is going to Vietnam to get out of Washington." The Republicans got "thumped" in the mid-term elections, largely due to the public's disdain for Bush's war in Iraq.

How much irony can we take?

Letter 54

Postmarked June 4, 1968.

As I open this letter, a black and white close-up picture of Donn's face drops out. He is wearing sunglasses. He is smiling slightly. He has on Army fatigues, and I can see the chain which holds his dogtags. The dimple in his left cheek is showing, so that it looks as if he is about to break into a big grin.

3 June

Hello Sweet girls,

How do you like the hilarious pix? Shaved it off right after this was taken as it was too hot and dirty.

[I look again at the photo. Yes, there is a light mustache and is that a little tiny beard?]

What does "S.A." stand for? Sex Appeal? Forgot Ocusol came in glass only—oh well, I've given up on contacs until Sept anyway.

Let me know what happens to David Smith. Glad to hear he got a "Poor Man's Porsche."

Evelyn Sweet-Hurd

What did you do with my insurance dividend?

How do you like the poster, Dockie? I thought it was hilarious.

I used one of the starlight scopes when I was an FO for the ARVN's last Nov. Didn't realize they were made in Roanoke. They really work well—the slang term we use is 'Glow-worm.'

Sorry this is such a dull letter but I'm bushed and must get some sleep.

Toodle,
D--------poo

§§§§§§§§§

I look in the envelope again. Yes, there is a folded piece of paper, and on one side is a "Wanted" poster with a portrait of a long-haired, bearded man.

Reward

For information leading to the apprehension of
Jesus Christ

Wanted—for sedition, criminal anarchy, vagrancy, and conspiring to overthrow the established government Dresses poorly, said to be a carpenter by trade, ill-nourished, has visionary ideas, associates with

common working people the unemployed and bums.
Alien—believed to be a Jew. Alias: 'Prince of Peace,'
Son of Man—'Light of the World' &c &c.
Professional agitator

Red beard, marks on hands and feet the result of
injuries inflicted by an angry mob led by respectable
citizens and legal authorities.

'Twas Ever Thus
Art Young Seattle PROVO 1967

On the back of this poster, a letter from James
Warburg to the NY Times [December 31, 1966]
regarding his opposition to the War in Vietnam and six
paragraphs from a group called "Promoting Enduring
Peace, Inc." from Woodmont, CT.

I scan these pieces. Warburg states that "It is
admittedly not easy for a proud nation to admit a
serious mistake in judgment...." The paragraphs from
"Promoting Enduring Peace" include quotes from
Neibuhr, U Thant, Harry S. Truman, Observateur , and
The Christian Century. Neibuhr says the Vietnam War
is "a fantastic adventure of United States imperialism
in an Asian civil war." Truman, according to this
source, stated on January 18, 1967, that "War is
fruitless, senseless, and a tragic adventure" in which
"there are no victors—only victims....War is a disease
and should be treated as such."

The call for an immediate end of the bombing of North Vietnam is made.

Did Donn find these pieces "hilarious," too, or just the "Wanted" poster for Jesus?

Letter 55

Postmark blurred.

Stationery is different, to say the least. Notepaper is decorated with a cartoon character and these words are at the top: KEEP SMILING!!
IT MAKES PEOPLE WONDER WHAT YOU'VE BEEN UP TO

10 June

Hello T & D,

Received your letters of the 2nd and 5th last nite. Really enjoyed the pix of Flo Sweet. How come you aren't going to use your newly acquired knowledge, Toombs? Sounds kind of dumb to me.

Gene still there? Well, Dockie, how's your trauma developing. Hope Gene and Joe haven't turned 1948 Walmann into an abattoir. (Neatsy word, yes?)

Is anybody working in that household this summer? Egad, I hope so.

Bye the bye, what's happening in the U.S.? Sounds like mass chaos. C'est dommage about RFK. Politics is too dangerous these days. The typical reaction over here was, "Guess we'd better take our flak jackets and steel pots home with us."

Sent my paper work to Ft Benning in hopes that they'll move my furniture before Sept. Any packages I send home you should open to see if they contain anything that will dry rot or mildew. I'll be sending some packages to Joan as it will mean I won't have to transport the stuff from Va. To Ga.

The weather is still hot and dusty. Oh, how I long to go home (hum along with Donnypoo).

Question. Dear Eng-maj type sister, which is correct: The can of soda is (laying or lying) in the freezer. Laying, yes? Because you placed or put it there. Please advise as we have a rather large dispute going on over here about it. Ta-ta.

How's Patti? Is she happy? How about a Polaroid of her with her new license plate? How's her clutch? Battery? TIRES?? Will she need new shoes by Sept? Ugh, I hope not, but fear the opposite.

Must run,
Luv and knishes,
SOT and/or BOD

P.S. What size tires does she use?

Letter 56

No envelope.

21 June

Hello T & D,

Well, all hell broke loose here yesterday. First of all, the colonel decided to completely change the command positions in the SVC Battery, so.... Cpt Kruse became S-2, the First Sergeant left and I am now with Alpha Battery as an F.O. Then about 4:30 PM the NVA shelled us and hit the ammo dump. The ensuing fire and explosions lasted about 8 hours. It was spectacular.

Tomorrow I leave for an F.O. assignment with a unit from the 1st Cavalry. I will be with the 3rd of the 5th Armored Cav which operates along the coast. It ought to be interesting and I hope to get some good pictures.

Send my mail to "A" Btry 1/40 ARTY and they'll forward it to me about once every 7 days.

I may go to Hong Kong on 22 July – depends on kismet, I guess.

Evelyn Sweet-Hurd

You may have read about the enemy aircraft sightings up here. We think we saw MIGS but some sightings were of helicopters. Oh, well.

The weather here is very hot.

This damn pen is leaking so I'll quit for now. Take care and I'll write again soon.

Luv,
Donniepoo

§§§§§§§§§

On the 21st of June he thinks he may go to Hong Kong on the 22nd of July.

He was killed in action July 25th.

He thought it would depend on kismet.

Letter 57

No envelope.

25 June

Good morning Toombs and Doc,

It's now 0638 and I'm sitting in my APC (Armored Personnel Carrier) waiting for the CO to give the word to move out. I'm with the 3/5 Armored Cav of the 9th Division which is operating along the coast east and south of Quang Tri city. During the day we 'search and destroy' and at night we set up ambush positions. This unit is really great. We have 3 tanks and 9 APCs per platoon and each APC is armed with 3 .50 cal machine guns and other jazz. So, we are heavily armed and extremely mobile.

I really enjoy being here because the action is plentiful and I like being on the offense. I call in artillery only when things really get nasty—so most of the time I just ride around with the CO and take pictures and fire my .50 cal from time to time.

The disadvantages to this job are: we're always dirty and hot, no latrines available, and the Gooks are clever at setting booby traps, and no mail.

Anyhow, I'm fine and enjoying myself immensely.

Thanx for the pix of D & G. Dockie, you really are looking good. What are you doing these days?

How's Patti? What do you call Gene's TR4? Tucus? What size tires does Patti have on now?

Don't forget to save a newspaper for me on 14 July.

Hard to believe that within 90 days I'll be going to school. Seems like years away. I wonder how hard it will be to readjust to that life.

The heat here is very high. What with the bad food (C's) and hot weather I've lost too much weight. Wish I could have an honest milk shake.

Well, must get my stuff together.
Take care and write soon,
Toodle,
Me

Letter 58

Postmarked July 4, 1968.
2 July

Hello T & D,

Received about 6 of your letters yesterday so will comment on those first. Toombs, how's your tooth and general health? How did Patti behave on her trip south? What size tires does she have now? Thanx for the grammatical ruling, Dockie. Must admit I'm rather thick at times. I don't remember Jim T. Have you had the oil changed lately? Bet she needs it.

I have so much to tell y'all about my recent activities as an FO but there's no place to sit down and write comfortably. Right now I'm squatting in the sand and the wind is blowing about 25 -30 mph. The weather is hot and windy.

I will be in Hong Kong from 22-27 July. Nice BD gift for me, yes?

As you know, I'm an FO for A troop 3 of the 5th Cav which is part of the 9th Inf Div. The 27th of June we got into a fight at Binh An (along the coast about 5 miles east of Dong Ha) with a Battalion of NVA. It was really something. After 3 days of close fighting we had killed 243, captured 44 while losing 7 dead and 12 wounded. We also had a tank blown up.

I took many many slides (hope they come out OK) and am anxious to see them. During the afternoon of the 27th, that night and most of the next day I called in jet strikes, naval gunfire and artillery. By the time we went in on foot we had 5 companies. I really enjoyed myself and received credit for 2 kills. Took pix of them. Anyway I'm very happy with this unit as we keep very busy and see a lot of action.

The living conditions are, of course, terrible and we stay dirty and messy 90% of the time.

Within 60 days I should be flying home—great thought, eh?

Plan to get many clothes while in H.K. Anything special either of you want?

Anyhoo, things are going fairly well here and hope they are the same with you.

Write soon and let me know what's new.
Toodle,
D----------------poo

P.S. If I get a good buy in HK I may buy some tires for Patti.

§§§§§§§§§

I have only three letters left to open.

As I ponder letter 58, postmarked July 4th, I have some trouble recognizing my brother. Either I didn't know him as well as I thought I did, or he had changed dramatically.

He received credit for 2 kills. He took pictures of them. He is very happy.

His birthday will be July 14, and it is family tradition that we save a newspaper commemorating Donn's birthday.

We saved one for July 14, 1968.

That was the last one.

Letter 59

No envelope.

8 PM
8 July

Hello D & T,

Another day less here in VietNasty and I'm thrilled. Bad news, they cancelled my R&R so I guess I'll have to scratch those plans. C'est la Army.

Received your BD card today, Toombie. Many thanx. Enjoyed Greg Gregory's article on the draft. Sure hope he's convicted and gets 5 years.

The weather remains very hot and dry. The action continues to be light although today we had a VC walk up and surrender to us-- very interesting.

Well, too much is happening here right now so I'll quit for now.

Tues morning—

Ah, another glorious day here amongst the flies and leeches-- only about 55 left. Not too much to report right now—I seem to have lost all desire to write-- As a matter of fact can't think of a thing to write about as I haven't seen a paper or magazine in 2 weeks. Did you see the July issue of Playboy—how did you like the interview with Paul Newman? Note his preference of cars.

Toodle,
D--------poo

Letter 60

No envelope.

Birthday Boy

Hi T & D!

Just a quick missive to thank you for the cards and letters. Tell Joan I got her cake and it was delish.

Yesterday I returned to Dong Ha—very sorry to leave that unit. Tomorrow I go out with the ARVN's. We will be operating in the area west of the Rockpile – will be gone for 1 – 2 weeks. It will be a physically demanding journey.

Still no word on what lies ahead after that. Since I'll be walking over hill and dale etc I won't get a chance to write so please drop a note to H & V, Cindy E. and Joan expressing my thanx for their BD greetings and why I can't write now—have much to do and little time.

Do take care and much love to you both.
Donn

§§§§§§§§§§

Our birthday boy wrote his last letter to my mother and me on July 14, 1968.

He was 26 years old that day.

I have been teaching English too many years, perhaps, showing my students how to find meaning in language, but I cannot read some of letter 60 without gasping:

"Still no word on what lies ahead after that."

And "have much to do and little time."

He signs this one with his name, not a cutesy version of his name or a silly pseudonym. He writes,

"Do take care and much love to you both."

Donn

Letter 61

Return address is LT Sweet 05424 509, A BTRY
1/40th ARTY,
APO San Francisco 96269. No postmark.
Addressed to: HOVE, 112 Swan Street, Scotia, New
York 12302

23 July

Hello SportsFans and/or HOVE Inc.,

Greetings from Northwest S. Vietnam. As you may
know I'm currently living in country-style splendor on
a picturesque mtn. top situated north of Khe Sahn
about two and a half miles. We left the Rockpile on 15
July and went west about 15 kilometers thru the most
obnoxious country imagineable. The Vietnamese
Army prefers to go straight up and straight down
mountains instead of traversing. It all added up to
agony, but "good training" as they say. We have H2O
and food dropped into us every 2 days—loverly. I
smell not unlike a river rat.

Tomorrow they lift us off of this mtn top and take us
about 10 km southeast to a point above CaLu where
we'll act as a blocking force for a Marine Bn coming
north. We've had rather light contact and it hasn't been

too bad casualty-wise.

Today we got writing supplies so that's why you're so lucky (p.s. Joke) to hear from me. Yesterday I scribbled a note to Toombie and Dockie on a used envelope.

Many, many thanx for the Johnny Walker Black Label-- y'all are very kind to nephew Donniepoo. When I get back to Dong Ha sometime in Aug I plan to devour the adorable bottle, label and all.

Unfortunately, it doesn't look like I'll get a second R&R, but c'est la guerre.

How are things with the business? Don't work too hard Uncle Viv and Aunt Howie; I have found that it's too traumatic.

Well, it's starting to rain so I better get this in an envelope and into my pack ASAP.

Luv,
Bernie Baruch

§§§§§§§§§

The last letter we have is this one, written to my aunt and uncle.

Look, Hemingway fans: It was starting to rain.

WESTERN UNION

TELEGRAM

221P EDT JUL 27 68 CTA 103 BB241
B SAA 008 XV GOVT PDB 4 EXTRA FAX
WASHINGTON DC 27 NFT
MRS MARION SWEET, DONT PHONE, DONT
DLR BETWEEN 10 PM AND 6 AM
1948 WALMANN RD ROANOKE VIR
THE SECRETARY OF THE ARMY HAS ASKED
ME TO EXPRESS HIS DEEP REGRET THAT
YOUR SON, FIRST LIEUTENANT DONN L.
SWEET DIED IN VIETNAM ON 25 JUL 68 AS A
RESULT OF WOUNDS RECEIVED WHILE ON
COMPAT OPERATION WHEN HIT BY
FRAGMENTS FROM HOSTILE MORTAR.
PLEASE ACCEPT MY DEEPEST SYMPATHY.
THIS CONFIRMS PERSONAL NOTIFICATION
MADE BY A REPRESENTATIVE OF THE
SECRETARY OF THE ARMY
KENNETH G WICKHAM MAJOR GENERAL USA
F-13 THE ADJUTANT GENERAL

WESTERN UNION

TELEGRAM

1014A EDT AUG 8 68 CTA 063 PC045
P DRA038 XV GOVT PDB 9 EXTRA FAX DOVER
AFB DEL 8 941A EDT
MRS MARION SWEET, REPORT DLY, DLY
GNTD, REPORT CHARGES
1948 WALMANN RD ROANOKE VIR
REMAINS 1LT DONN L SWEET ARRIVE
ALBANY NY 11:30 AM 9 AUG ON
MO FLT 33 MABEE & BERNING FUNERAL
HOME NOTIFIED
COMMANDER DOVER AFB DELAWARE 14-8

11:30 AM 9 33 14-8
(946).

Postmortem

What would you like to see of the postmortem items?

Here is a document from the Army stating that on 5 July 1968 LT Sweet had suggested that 105 mm Cannisters be ordered and that the Army was considering that suggestion.

There are several letters to my mother from U.S. Senators expressing deep regret and reminding her that her son gave his life for freedom and for peace.

Oh, and one of the letters was addressed to Mrs. Donn Sweet. Yes, State Senator Clarence Bell of Pennsylvania took the time to handwrite:

Please accept my deepest sympathy for the loss of your brave son in Viet Nam in the defense of freedom. Most sincerely yours, Clarence D. Bell, State Senator.

If only someone in Clarence Bell's office had noted that Mrs. Donn Sweet was the ex-wife of LT Donn Sweet, not his mother.

Here's a note from someone in the Military Mail Terminal, San Francisco. It is addressed to the wrong house number. And it reads:

Dear Sir:

The inclosed [sic] mail, addressed to 1 LT Donn L. Sweet, bears your return address.

Official records of the Department of the Army, as of 28 July 1968, indicate that he was reported to have deceased on 25 July 1968.

I regret that it was not possible to have delivered this mail to him.

Sincerely, Thomas C Adams

Back in my angry days, I might be offended by this. LTC, AGC Adams regrets that it was not possible to have delivered this mail to my brother? You seem to have missed a larger point, LTC, AGC Adams. And I am sure my mother loved being addressed as "Dear Sir."

§§§§§§§§§

Here's a long fairly lengthy letter from General William Westmoreland. General Westmoreland writes that Donn *"has given the priceless gift of life to protect his loved ones at home and to safeguard the cherished beliefs for which his Nation stands."*

I am wondering now what the families of people killed in Iraq are reading.

§§§§§§§§§

Here's a letter from Lyndon B. Johnson. He and Mrs. Johnson have us in their prayers, he says.

§§§§§§§§§

On August 8, 1968, a medic named James Williams wrote this:

Dear Mrs. Sweet,

Your son (Lt.) Donn Sweet, was truly a good friend and I will always remember him. I am lost for words at this time. I do wish to express my heartfilled sympathy to you and your family. You have my prayers. In sympathy,

Sp/4 James Williams, Medic, 1/40 Arty, Republic Viet Nam

§§§§§§§§§

From the University of Georgia School of Law, Professor John Murray writes a nice letter that expresses a good deal of distress for the loss of the young man who was to have been in school there within the next month.

Evelyn Sweet-Hurd

§§§§§§§§§§

Here are two letters from men who served with Donn:

Department of the Army
Headquarters 108th Artillery Group
APO San Francisco 96269

11 Aug 1968

Dear Mrs. Sweet:

I want to express to you my heartfelt sympathy over the death of your son, First Lieutenant Donn L. Sweet. We share your loss, for we too are grieved over his death.

Your son was well-liked and respected by the members of his unit. We are proud of the cheerful and conscientious manner which he performed his duties, and of the contribution he made to the defense of freedom in a troubled world. While this does not bring him back to you, I hope you will find some satisfaction and solace in knowing that he did his job well.....

David L. Jones, Colonel, Artillery

11 Aug 1968

Dear Mrs. Sweet:

It is difficult for me to express the sorrow felt by the officers and men of this battalion over the recent death of your son, First Lieutenant Donn L. Sweet, United States Army.

Your son was critically wounded in the late afternoon of 25 July 1968 while on a search and destroy operation with the Second Regiment, Army of the Republic of Vietnam. Your son was serving as the artillery forward observer for the unit and was attempting to call for an artillery strike against a Viet Cong/North Vietnamese force which they had encountered. An enemy mortar attack commenced on the position which your son and the members of his forward observer team had occupied. During this attack, your son was critically wounded by an enemy mortar round which exploded a short distance from him. He was immediately moved from the area and evacuated by helicopter to D Medical Company, 3rd Medical Battalion Hospital at Dong Ha. Enroute to the hospital, your son died without ever regaining consciousness.

Donn's personal belongings are now being readied for shipment and will be forwarded to you shortly. A memorial service will be held in the battery where your son served with skill and courage. Pictures of this service will be forwarded to you upon completion of the processing. In the meantime if I can be of assistance to you in any way please do not hesitate to write me.

While I realize that my words cannot lessen the deep sorrow that I know you must feel at this time, I do hope you will gain some comfort from that knowledge that your son gave his life in defense of the freedoms enjoyed by all of us today.

Sincerely,
Lawrence H.D. Williams
LTC, Arty
Commanding

Record of Personal Property—Combat Areas

Sweet, Donn L. 1 LT 05 424 509

Inventory of property from the US Army Mortuary Vietnam

1 Pr. Tan shorts civ
1 book The Lawyers
1 flash light
5 handkerchiefs
1 overnight bag
1 pocket knife
1 novelty doll
49 envelopes
1 pr. Shoe trees
4 tooth brushes
3 rolls of film
1 pr. Sun glasses w/case
1 film ultima
1 view graph argus
1 soap dish
1 btl baby powder
1 35 mm camera SN 226545
2 comb
2 polar lenses Kodak
1 nail clip w/case
1 t-shirt
1 sewing kit box
1 pr. Glasses w/case
2 4-cent stamps

1 pk 8-cent stamps
1 name plate plastic
1 Lt. bar
2 wash cloths
1 Arty ins.
1 shaving kit
17 cards and letters
38 pictures
2 large pictures
5 credit cards
1 Playboy club card
1 Bank account ID card
7 Bank check books
1 address book
1 DA form 1341
1 DD form 1101
2 Kodak prepaid processing mailer
1 Red Cross Blood Donor card
9 negatives
1 military card
1 yellow note book
1 camera manual
1 box color slides
1 8 mm Kodak camera w/case
1 ring gold in color
1 dictionary
1 Swappy dog
1 civ belt
2 civ shirts
1 jacket
1 garrison cap

1 turtle neck shirt
2 towels
12 socks
2 pr civ trousers
1 water repellant pants
1 Hong Konh nite light
1 memo pad
1 bowl
1 nail clipper
1 shoe brush
1 Awol bag
1 Alpurpose bag
1 red sweat shirt
1 contact tube
1 pr low quarters
2 sets of khakis
///////////LAST ITEM//////////////////////

Evelyn Sweet-Hurd

I can only imagine what Joan and I may have written to the Army on August 1, 1968. Here is the response we received:

Department of the Army
Headquarters 1st Battalion 40th Artillery
APO San Francisco 96269

30 August 1968

Dear Ladies:

I received your letter, dated 1 August 1968, inquiring into the circumstances relative to your brother's death and apologize for the delay in answering. Enclosed you will find copies of two General Orders. General Order Number 3979 awarding Donn the Silver Star for gallantry in action will help you to better understand what actions took place on the day of his death. I wish to tell you that the Silver Star is the nation's third highest award for heroism. The Medal of Honor and the Distinguished Service Cross are the only awards for heroism which rank higher than the medal which Donn received posthumously. General Order Number 3937, awarded Donn the Bronze Star Medal for meritorious service. This award is the United States Army's third highest award for service. In addition to these two coveted awards, Donn was also awarded the Purple Heart, Vietnam Campaign Medal, the Vietnam Service Medal with two campaign stars, and the National Defense Service Medal.

230

I can only add that the courage displayed by your brother on 25 July 1968, is reason for you to always be proud of Donn. Having known your brother personally, I have the highest esteem and praise for him as do his fellow officers and men of the 40th Artillery. He gave his life in attempting to aid his fellow man, and in doing so, placed himself in all our minds as a man to be emulated by free men everywhere…..

Lawrence H.D. Williams
LTC, Arty
Commanding

Evelyn Sweet-Hurd

15 August 1968

Award of the Silver Star

The following AWARD is announced posthumously.

Sweet, Donn L. First Lieutenant Artillery

US Army, Battery A, 1st Battalion, 40th Artillery, 108th Artillery Group

Date action: 25 July 1968

Theater: Republic of Vietnam

Reason: For gallantry in action while engaged in military operations involving conflict with an armed hostile force in the Republic of Vietnam: First Lieutenant Sweet distinguished himself by exceptionally valorous actions on 25 July 1968 as an artillery forward observer on a combat operation. During the late afternoon, he was helilifted into an enemy infested area. The enemy had already inflicted numerous casualties on the two Vietnamese companies which had already been inserted into the landing zone. Immediately upon departing the aircraft, LT Sweet came under intense automatic weapons fire. Knowing that he must reach higher ground to more effectively adjust the friendly fire and air strikes, he unhesitantly ran forward to the base of a ridge leading to a suitable observation post. Enroute, he came under enemy sniper fire. Advancing to within fifty yards of the enemy, Lieutenant Sweet killed the sniper with rifle fire. He continued up the ridge until he reached the crest of the hill. Despite the position's lack of cover and concealment, he decided to remain there to attempt to eliminate the enemy resistance with artillery fire. As he began to adjust the supporting fire, his position was hit by an enemy mortar shell, mortally wounding him. First Lieutenant Sweet's gallantry in action, at the cost of his life, was in keeping with the highest traditions of the military service and reflects great credit upon himself, his unit and the United States Army.

Authority: By direction of the President under the provisions of the Act of Congress, approved 9 July 1918

Robert C. Taber
Brigadier General, US Army
Chief of Staff

Summer, 2006

This Spring, I went with my daughter Caitlin to get my very first pedicure.

Sitting in that salon, I noted that all of the employees were Vietnamese. I decided to try my wings.

I began to try to chat with the technicians who were working on our feet. The young woman who was working with Caitlin spoke quite a bit of English; the young woman who was massaging my feet and showing me nail colors was less fluent.

I asked the pedicurists when they had come from Vietnam. About ten years ago, they said. No, they had not known each other before coming to work at this nail salon in Conyers, GA, but they were coincidentally from the same part of Vietnam.

A little boy about 4 years old came running over to the young woman who was about to paint my toenails. He was adorably cute, and she gave him a hug before sending him over to watch "Sponge Bob Squarepants" on the DVD player they had in the room.

I asked her what his name was.

"Tom," she said with a shy smile.

She told me Tom was getting ready to enter kindergarten, and that she hoped he would be able to help her with her English.

I asked her what part of Vietnam she was from.
She and her colleague worked together to tell me that they were from a part that was neither a big city nor a rural area, and that I probably would not know it.

"Is it around Dong Ha?" I asked.

The women dropped their formality and their faces lit up. With big smiles, they asked, "Yes! You know Dong Ha?"

Oh, yes, I replied. My brother was killed in Vietnam.

"Oh," they said somberly.

It was then that I noticed the art work on the technicians' fingernails. The one applying color to Caitlin's toenails had bright flowers on her fingernails. And the one who had been struggling with the calluses on my older, never-before-pedicured feet, had fingernails with red, white, and blue artwork, art of the American flag.

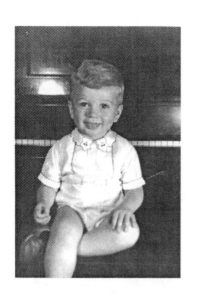

Donn Lafayette Sweet
July 14, 1942 – July 25, 1968

Printed in the United States
119832LV00001B/49/A